LEASEHOLD MANAGEMENT: A GOOD PRACTICE GUIDE

PETER ROBINSON

WITH ADDITIONAL MATERIAL BY JOHN MILLS

CHARTERED INSTITUTE OF HOUSING

NATIONAL HOUSING FEDERATION

AND THE HOUSING CORPORATION

The Chartered Institute of Housing

The Chartered Institute of Housing is the professional organisation for all people who work in housing. Its purpose is to maximise the contribution that housing professionals make to the well-being of communities. The Institute has more than 17,000 members working in local authorities, housing associations, the private sector and educational institutions.

Chartered Institute of Housing
Octavia House, Westwood Way
Coventry CV4 8JP
Tel: 024 7685 1700 Fax: 024 7669 5110
Website: www.cih.org

National Housing Federation

The National Housing Federation is the trade body for 1,400 housing associations that build, regenerate and manage affordable housing for all. Across the country, Federation members work with and on behalf of local people to create places where people want to live, by making a fresh commitment – to neighbourhoods, to customers and to excellence. In 2003 the National Housing Federation launched *iN business for neighbourhoods*, a national alliance of housing associations working to create successful neighbourhoods in cities, towns and villages across England.

National Housing Federation
175 Gray's Inn Road
London WC1X 8UP
Tel: 020 7278 6571 Fax: 020 7833 8323
Website: www.housing.org.uk

The Housing Corporation

The Housing Corporation is the government agency which registers, regulates and funds over 2,000 social landlords in England, which between them provide around 1.5 million homes for people in need. The Corporation has an important role as a promoter of good practice in the social housing sector.

The Housing Corporation
149 Tottenham Court Road
London W1T 7BN
Tel: 020 7393 2000 Fax: 020 7393 2111
Website: www.housingcorp.gov.uk

Leasehold Management: A Good Practice Guide
Written by Peter Robinson
© Chartered Institute of Housing, the National Housing Federation and the Housing Corporation 2003
ISBN: 1-903208-52-1

Layout by Jeremy Spencer
Cover illustration by Warwicks UK Ltd
Printed by Genesis Print and Marketing

CONTENTS

About the Authors

Peter Robinson

Peter is a partner in housing consultancy PRHC. Before becoming a consultant in 1990, he was Assistant Director of Housing in the London Borough of Greenwich.

He has worked with senior Government officials, and Housing Corporation staff on both operational and strategic matters, as well as health authorities, planning authorities and the commercial development sector.

He is a board member of the London and Quadrant Housing Group and of Tower Homes and is Chair of Quadrant Supported Living.

PRHC are recognised experts on home ownership management – Peter and Rona Nicholson having written the CIH/NHF Good Practice Guide *Leasehold Management for Social Landlords* published in 1996.

PRHC also wrote the recommended Leasehold Performance Standards and Performance Indicators published in the CIH *Housing Management Standards Manual* and have written several publications on low cost homeownership for the National Housing Federation.

The consultancy has also undertaken many assignments for individual landlords in relation to reviewing and developing their home ownership management services, providing resident advice and consultation, undertaking satisfaction surveys and providing training for leasehold managers and other staff.

PRHC assembled the initial set of good practice examples in respect of sales and leasehold management published by HouseMark and have delivered workshops on various aspects of leasehold management for the CIH.

PRHC: Tel: 020 8460 6353 email: info@prhc.org.uk Website: prhc.org.uk

John Mills

John has extensive experience of leasehold management in both the private and social housing sectors, having worked for Anchor, Hanover and Peverel.

He co-wrote and promoted the first Code of Practice on Leasehold Management to be adopted under the Leasehold Reform, Housing and Urban Development Act 1993 and was a member of the Government working group considering the leasehold reforms introduced in the Commonhold and Leasehold Reform Act 2002. He is also a member of the South West Rent Assessment Panel, and has acted as expert witness at Leasehold Valuation Tribunals.

John is part-time Policy Officer of the Association of Retirement Housing Managers. As an independent consultant he has been engaged in researching, developing, writing and introducing policy and procedures for leasehold management and sheltered housing management.

FOREWORD

Managing leaseholders' homes has always been a complex and demanding area of work, requiring rigorous attention to detail, well-organised procedures and a scrupulously fair-minded approach. Currently leasehold managers face new challenges in implementing the provisions of the Commonhold and Leasehold Reform Act 2002 and its related Commencement Orders and Regulations.

This new guide, written as the second Commencement Order of the 2002 Act comes into force, explains the current legal and regulatory framework for leasehold management. It examines the new requirements for consulting leaseholders, explains the new role of Leasehold Valuation Tribunals, and looks in detail at many other aspects of delivering the service, including the annual service charge cycle, administering sales, and maximising leaseholders' options where regeneration schemes are being planned.

The Housing Corporation and Broomleigh Housing Association are very pleased to sponsor this guide, and recommend it to leasehold managers and to leaseholders' representatives and their advisers as a comprehensive source of information. We are delighted that the guide has broken new ground by presenting good practice information for leasehold managers in the social sector and the private sector within the same publication. We welcome the joint working between the Chartered Institute of Housing, the National Housing Federation and the Housing Corporation to develop and co-publish the guide, and appreciate the many contributions made by other organisations and individuals who provided advice, suggestions and support.

Peter Dixon – *Chairman, The Housing Corporation*
Simon Randall – *Chairman, Broomleigh Housing Assocation Ltd*

ACKNOWLEDGEMENTS

CIH and the NHF would like to thank the Housing Corporation for providing an Innovation and Good Practice Grant to fund this publication, and to thank Broomleigh Housing Association for further sponsorship.

The project team is indebted to the many organisations and individuals who provided encouragement and feedback on drafts of the guide, including AIMS, ALG, ARMA, The Audit Commission, Birmingham City Council, Boleyn & Forest HA, Roger Brayshaw (consultant), Brighton & Hove Council, Bromford Housing Group, Hightown Praetorian Housing Association, LGA, LB Waltham Forest, NHF Home Ownership Advisory Panel, John Paterson (leaseholder), Portsmouth City Council, Retirement Lease Housing Association, Salisbury DC and Westminster City Council.

Especially helpful input was given by Rafael Runco (Independent Housing Ombudsman Scheme), Darren Tierney (then at ODPM) and Peter Haler (LEASE). Chris Baines, Chairman of the Institute of Residential Property Managers, has provided valuable advice and support throughout the project.

Nick Barnard and Caroline Cowley of Owen White Solicitors in Slough checked the legal content of the text, and Paula Robinson of PRHC contributed to research and drafting material. Thanks are also due to Rona Nicholson, co-author of the 1996 Good Practice Guide *Leasehold Management for Social Landlords* for helping to lay the foundations for that guide and for commenting on this new one.

CHAPTER 1

INTRODUCTION

This chapter provides an overview of the leasehold housing sector and includes sources of further guidance for leasehold managers, landlords and managing agents.

❏ 1.1 The leasehold housing sector

This new guide is written for both public and private sector landlords and managing agents.

Since publication of the original version of the guide, which was aimed mainly at the public sector, the profile of leasehold management within many public sector landlord organisations has grown, and the emphasis that was given in that guide to getting the right organisational approach and level of corporate commitment to effective leasehold management seems to have been heeded. However it has led to a stronger desire for clear guidance on a wide range of technical and legal matters affecting leaseholds, a need that is equally felt within the private sector.

As well as changes to the legislative framework within which leaseholds must be created and managed, there have been important Leasehold Valuation Tribunal decisions of which leasehold managers need to be aware, and developments in good practice particularly around leaseholder consultation, information and involvement.

The Commonhold and Leasehold Reform Act 2002 has introduced important changes to the law on service charges and leaseholder consultation, as well as clarifying and extending leaseholders' rights in other respects, although many of these changes will not come fully into effect until 2004.

Leaseholders themselves are also becoming increasingly aware of their rights, and some leasehold management weaknesses that landlords have been able to ignore in the past now have to be addressed by managers, who often find themselves working within organisations lacking the knowledge and infrastructure to properly support them.

The Audit Commission now has responsibility for inspecting the leasehold management services of both local authorities and housing associations. This will focus attention on differing practices and failures to comply with the law, leases and standards of good practice across the social housing sector.

These factors have influenced the balance of this new guide. The original good practice guide dealt comprehensively with organisational and corporate policy around leasehold management – the new guide addresses the burgeoning need for easily accessible information on how to deal with a wide range of practical problems.

The aim has been to increase the technical content in a readable way.

❑ 1.2 Signposts to good practice and further guidance

It would be impossible in a guide of this length to provide answers to every question that a leasehold manager or leaseholder may have. Indeed there are many other publications that address particular areas of interest to the leasehold manager in comprehensive detail.

This guide sets out to identify the sources of further information the leasehold manager will need. This is done through:
- A list of essential basic reading at the end of this chapter
- Details of other key general sources of information that need to be available in the leasehold management office for staff to refer to – also given at the end of this chapter
- Lists of key further references at the end of each chapter

As well as providing extensive leasehold management guidance, the guide provides leasehold managers, leasehold management students and leaseholders with a single point of initial reference, from which they can identify and access further information.

❑ 1.3 The scale and nature of leasehold tenure

The Survey of English Housing 1998/99 indicates that leasehold tenure comprises approximately 12% of all owner-occupied homes, or 1.8 million households, of which approximately one million are flats and 800,000 are houses.

85% of those leasehold flats are concentrated in the South of England with 47% in Greater London alone, whilst leasehold houses are mainly concentrated in the North West (58%).

As might be expected there are distinct differences between leaseholds in the wholly private sector and leaseholds in the current or former social housing sector.

The freehold interest in leasehold flats in the private sector is much more likely to be owned jointly by leaseholders themselves, with nearly 40% managing without any professional help. Managing agents look after a further 47%, of which some two thirds have been appointed by landlords, and one third by leaseholders who jointly own their freehold.

Around 20% of all leasehold flats were formerly in the social rented sector, the majority owned by local authorities, which continue to provide the management service. 89% of these are in the south of England, with 51% in London.

Around two thirds of leaseholds in the social sector are still owned by the former tenants of those flats, but the remaining third have been sold on and this proportion is growing fast, particularly in London and the South East.

Leasehold occupation of local authority and housing association homes arises through a number of different routes. Each route leads to a different set of leasehold characteristics which affect the management tasks involved and the nature of the relationship between leaseholder and landlord.

For example, flats sold under the Right To Buy by local authorities are usually scattered within blocks also partly occupied by periodic tenants, whereas shared ownership leaseholders live predominantly in purpose built schemes; leaseholders in schemes for the elderly have often been owner occupiers elsewhere; leaseholders under the Right to Buy, Preserved Right to Buy or Right to Acquire schemes will previously have been sitting periodic tenants of the freeholder.

In the private sector there is greater variety of property type and value, with more found in purpose-built leasehold schemes than in the public sector.

❏ 1.4 The range of leasehold types covered by the guide

The guide applies to both private and public sector leaseholds – specifically:
- Residential long leases (21 years or more at commencement)
- House and flat leases
- Leases granted under the Right to Buy and Preserved Right to Buy
- Leases granted under the Right to Acquire and Voluntary Purchase Grant
- Shared ownership leases
- Retirement leases and leasehold schemes for the elderly

The application of Landlord and Tenant Law and Housing Law varies according to the type of leasehold, and these differences are explained in the relevant chapters of the guide. The legislation applies to England and Wales only.

Although the guide is written primarily for leasehold managers it will also have relevance for the managers of periodic tenancies. As a result of rent restructuring in the social rented sector, landlords are now separating the charges for some services from the rent charged for those tenancies, so that where variable service charges already exist or are being introduced, some of the requirements of legislation described in the guide will also apply to them.

❏ 1.5 Treating leaseholders as customers

The guide aims to provide landlords and leasehold managers with the technical and good practice basis from which to meet the complex legal requirements of leasehold management while always regarding leaseholders as customers who have high expectations of good quality services and value for money.

The residential long leaseholder's interest in the property they occupy is substantially greater than that of their landlord or manager, and they look to their landlord to ensure that their interest is properly protected.

Many leasehold managers have recognised the need to treat leaseholders as customers with whom they need an effective working relationship. Modern approaches to customer care and the use of internet-based services provide both leaseholders and landlords with the potential to work together to plan, monitor and control the buildings in which they share major long term interests.

· ·

The **London Borough of Croydon** provides an excellent online leaseholders' guide covering the topics below.

The lease
- What is a lease?
- The leaseholder's main obligations
- The council's main obligations
- Deeds of Variation
- Extending the lease

Service charges
- What are service charges and why are they necessary?
- What do service charges pay for?
- How are they calculated?

- Collection of charges
- Queries about charges
- Summaries of costs
- Payment difficulties

Getting services
- Management and administration
- Estate management
- Maintenance
- Caretaking services
- Graffiti
- Nuisance
- Harassment
- Insurance
- Complaints
- Management audit
- Leasehold Valuation Tribunal

Major repairs and improvements
- What are major repairs and improvements?
- Limits to how much you may have to pay
- Deciding what needs doing
- Consultation – major repair and improvement programme
- Consultation – environmental improvements programme
- Querying major works
- Tendering the work and managing the contractors
- Help with repair costs
- Carrying out your own improvements

Selling, letting and buying the freehold
- Selling your home
- Repaying discounts
- 'Buy Back' schemes
- Subletting
- Buying the freehold

Keeping you informed and listening to your views
- Leasehold News
- Leaseholder surgeries
- Leaseholders' conference
- General consultation
- Leaseholders' Panel

It can be accessed at www.croydon.gov.uk/hsgdept/tenants/
Leaseholders_Guide.htm

❑ 1.6 Essential reading for leasehold managers

Association of Retirement Housing Managers (1996 – revised edition due spring 2004) *Code of Practice for Private Sheltered Housing* ISBN 0 952699 0 2
Statutory approval given under s87 Leasehold Reform, Housing and Urban Development Act 1993

Royal Institution of Chartered Surveyors (1997 – revised edition in progress) *Service Charge Residential Management Code* ISBN 0 85406 643 8
Statutory approval given under s87 Leasehold Reform, Housing and Urban Development Act 1993

Freedman, Philip, Shapiro, Eric & Slater, Brian (2002, 3rd edition) *Service Charges, Law and Practice* Jordan Publishing Ltd ISBN 0 85308 710 5

Rawson, Derek (2003) *Service Charges – A Guide for Registered Social Landlords* National Housing Federation

Housing Corporation (2003) *A Charter for Housing Association Applicants and Residents*

Housing Corporation *The Leaseholders Guarantee* (now out of date but compliance may be a contractual requirement of some leases)

Cox, Nigel (1993, 4th edition expected 2004) *Running a Flat Management Company* Jordan Publishing Ltd ISBN 0 85308 8608

Michaux, Steve (2003) *Principles of Council Leasehold Management*, Association of London Government
www.londonhousing.gov.uk/publication_list.asp

LEASE – information leaflets – check website for latest updated information
www.lease-advice.org.uk

ODPM booklets
Items marked * currently being updated to include the CLRA 2002 and will be available as one booklet

Commonhold and Leasehold Reform Act 2002 – Initial guidance on residential leasehold reform provisions (Dec 2002) HC 00459

Long Leaseholders – Your rights and responsibilities (Aug 2002) 02 HC 00437

Applying to a Leasehold Valuation Tribunal – Service charges, insurance, management (Aug 2002) 02 HC 00433*

Right of first refusal for long leaseholders and other tenants in privately owned flats (Aug 2002) 02 HC 00434*

Leasehold Houses – Your right to buy the freehold of your house or extend your lease (Aug 2002) 02 HC 00436*

Leasehold Flats – Your right to buy the freehold of your building or renew your lease (Aug 2002) 02 HC 00435*

Lease running out? – Security of tenure for long leaseholders (Aug 2000)*

❏ 1.7 Essential reference works for the leasehold management office

Arden and Partington, Hunter and Redpath-Stevens *Arden and Partington on Housing Law* Sweet and Maxwell (loose leaf volume – cd and online – subscription service) www.sweetandmaxwell.co.uk

Driscoll, James *Housing Law and Precedents* Sweet and Maxwell (loose leaf volume updated quarterly – subscription service – contains many useful forms and other documents as well as case law) www.sweetandmaxwell.co.uk

ODPM housing booklets – on the Right to Buy and other help to buy www.odpm.gov.uk

Kilcoyne, Desmond (1997) *Leaseholder Management* (Law and Practice in Social Housing – Arden's Housing Library) Lemos and Crane ISBN 1 898001 10 3

Henderson, Josephine (1997) *Rights to Buy and Acquire* (Law and Practice in Social Housing – Arden's Housing Library) Lemos and Crane ISBN 1 898001 19 7

❏ 1.8 Signposts to sources of further information

Office of the Deputy Prime Minister (ODPM) website for news and downloadable documents regarding leasehold issues, booklets www.housing.odpm.gov.uk/information/leaseholdreform

The Leasehold Advisory Service (LEASE) – an independent advice agency funded by government grant – various downloadable leaflets and information and guidance available including details of LVT decisions www.lease-advice.org.uk

The Association of Retirement Housing Managers (ARHM) – for Code of Practice, revised edition due spring 2004, also good practice notes for members www.arhm.org

The Association of Residential Managing Agents (ARMA) has a code of practice and provides information and guidance for its members www.arma.org.uk

The Housing Corporation (HC) – Regulatory Code and Guidance, circulars, information, inspection reports www.housingcorp.gov.uk

The Audit Commission – Best value review inspection reports and other information
www.audit-commission.gov.uk

The Chartered Institute of Housing (CIH) – professional body for those who work in housing – also produces publications and good practice information
www.cih.org

The National Housing Federation (NHF) – Housing association trade organisation – also produces publications and good practice information
www.housing.org.uk

The Royal Institution of Chartered Surveyors (RICS) – professional organisation for Chartered Surveyors – produces Code of Practice for service charge residential management and other residential management information
www.rics.org.uk

The Institute of Residential Property Managers – professional body for those who work in leasehold property management
www.irpm.org.uk

Commonhold and Leasehold Reform Act 2002 (CLRA 2002)
www.legislation.hmso.gov.uk/acts/acts2002/20020015.htm

HMSO – Public General Acts since 1988 – are available on the website
www.legislation.hmso.gov.uk

The Independent Housing Ombudsman Scheme (IHOS) – for 'digests' of selected cases, advice and annual reports
www.ihos.org.uk

Local Government Ombudsman
www.lgo.org.uk

The Law Commission
www.lawcom.gov.uk

The Local Government Association
www.lga.gov.uk

Association of London Government
www.alg.gov.uk

AIMS – impartial advice, information and mediation service for people living in and managing sheltered housing – rented and leaseholders – part of Age Concern
www.ageconcern.org.uk/aims

HOMES – shared ownership – details of new and resales properties – existing shared owners can use for resales with landlord's permission
www.homes.org.uk
The facilitated mobility service for shared ownership currently provided by HOMES is subject to change from 2004. Details on ODPM website.

Residential Property Tribunal Service (RPTS) – an independent body which gives an accessible service to landlords, tenants and leaseholders either to Rent Assessment Committees or the Leasehold Valuation Tribunal – various information and booklets can be downloaded
www.rpts.gov.uk

CHAPTER 2

THE LEGAL AND
REGULATORY FRAMEWORK

This chapter summarises the legislation, regulations, codes of practice and other sources of good practice about which landlords, leasehold managers and managing agents need to know.

It deals with the Landlord and Tenant Acts and Housing Acts, provides more detailed reference to the new requirements of the Commonhold and Leasehold Reform Act 2002, and shows which categories of landlord are affected by each provision in the new Act.

It refers to the regulatory, inspection and best value regimes with which local authority and most housing association landlords need to comply.

Further detail about legislative and regulatory provisions can be found in later chapters.

❏ 2.1 The legislative framework

Leasehold managers are faced with a legal framework that has evolved over many years and is now spread across several acts of Parliament as well as being significantly affected by case law. To make matters worse the most recent legislation provides little of the detail leasehold managers require, as this is contained in a series of Commencement Orders, issued at different times and subject to changes that may also be made at different times.

Readers in Wales should also be aware that Commencement Orders under the Commonhold and Leasehold Reform Act 2002 may have different operative dates from those applying in England.

In this chapter we have summarised the legislation, regulatory controls and other guidance with which residential leasehold managers should comply.

❑ 2.2 The principal legislation

The key legislation of which all leasehold managers need to be aware includes:
- The Landlord and Tenant Acts of 1985 and 1987
- The Leasehold Reform, Housing and Urban Development Act 1993
- The Housing Act 1996
- The Commonhold and Leasehold Reform Act 2002

It is important to note that the Commonhold and Leasehold Reform Act 2002 has introduced significant amendments to the other four Acts.

In addition public sector managers need to be aware of the Housing Act 1985 as it affects the Right to Buy, Preserved Right to Buy and the Right to Acquire. Important provisions also exist in the following:
- The Property Misdescriptions Act 1991
- The Consumer Protection Act 1987
- The Law of Property Act 1925
- The Unfair Terms in Contracts Regulations 1999

Private sector managing agents and some housing association managers also need to be fully aware of the basic requirements of company law.

The main matters covered in the legislation are summarised below and the main features of their application in practice are described in the subsequent chapters.

❑ 2.3 The main legislative provisions

See the Table on pages 12 and 13.

❑ 2.4 The Commonhold and Leasehold Reform Act 2002

■ Introduction
The Commonhold and Leasehold Reform Act 2002 will undoubtedly present leasehold managers with some major challenges simply as a result of the way it has been drafted. The Act itself cannot be used as a single point of reference as most of its clauses either amend previous legislation in a manner that requires reference back to the original legislation for the meaning of the amendment to become clear, or prepare the way for regulations yet to be finalised.

Part 1 of the Act introduces a new form of tenure known as Commonhold that will be available for new developments, and for conversion of existing freeholds where all the leaseholders involved agree to participate and buy out any freehold interests.

Legislation	Principal matters covered	Dealt with in chapter of this guide
Landlord and Tenant Act 1985	• Definition of a variable service charge	5
	• Definition of a tenant covered by the legislation	5
	• Reasonableness of service charges	6
	• Leaseholders' rights to consultation on repairs over a prescribed limit	7
	• The 18 month limit on charging for costs relating to service charges	5
	• Leaseholders' rights to inspect supporting accounts	5
	• Requesting information from a superior landlord	5
	• Failure to comply with these requests	5
	• Leaseholders' rights in relation to insurance matters	5
	• Recognising residents' associations	5
	• Rights of residents' associations to be consulted about the employment of managing agents	5
	• Right of First Refusal	5
Landlord and Tenant Act 1987	• Variation of leases	3
	• Obligation for private landlords to set up trust funds for service charge monies	5
	• Demands for rent and service charges must include landlord's name and address	5
Leasehold Reform, Housing and Urban Development Act 1993	• Leaseholders' rights to carry out a management audit	5
	• Leaseholders' rights to collective enfranchisement	8
	• Power of the Secretary of State for the Environment to approve Codes of Practice	2
	• Increased role for Leasehold Valuation Tribunals	11
Commonhold and Leasehold Reform Act 2002	See the more detailed summary that follows in Chapter 2.4 of this guide	
Housing Act 1980	• Limitation of RTB leaseholders' liability to pay for structural defects to the first 10 years	7

Legislation	Principal matters covered	Dealt with in chapter of this guide
Housing Act 1985	• Right to Buy for local authority and non-charitable housing association tenants • Requirements of the sales process • Limitations of leaseholders' liability to pay service charges in the first 5 years • The right to a loan for leaseholders under Housing (Service Charge Loans) Regulations 1992	4 4 4 5
Housing Act 1996	• Right to Acquire for tenants of Registered Social Landlords • Limitation on when forfeiture for non-payment of service charges can be sought • Increased role for Leasehold Valuation Tribunals • Increased scope for collective enfranchisement • Powers for Secretary of State to require reduction or waiver of service charges in certain circumstances	4 8 11 8 6
Property Misdescriptions Act 1991	Creates offence of providing misleading advice or information to purchasers	4
Consumer Protection Act 1987	Landlord's obligations not to give artificially low estimates of service charges	5
Housing and Planning Act 1986	Obligation for valuers to take into account 5 year estimates for service charges	4, 6
Financial Services and Markets Act 2000	Rules governing the provision of investment advice	4
Law of Property Act 1925	Forfeiture provisions and notices to mortgagees regarding relief from forfeiture	8
Arbitration Act 1996	Sets out powers of Arbitration Tribunals	8

This guide does not deal with the operation of Commonhold, although the right of leaseholders to convert to a Commonhold is dealt with in Chapter 8. The Housing Corporation is considering the potential application of Commonhold to future shared ownership schemes.

Part 2 of the Act contains important provisions that amend earlier legislation. These amendments are to:

- The Landlord and Tenant Act 1985 in respect of service charges
- The Leasehold Reform Housing and Urban Development Act 1993 in respect of collective enfranchisement and lease renewals
- The Landlord and Tenant Act 1987 in respect of the variation of leases
- The Law of Property Act 1925 and the Housing Act 1996 in respect of forfeiture for breach of a covenant or condition of a lease

The Act also introduces the Right to Manage for long leaseholders and extends the jurisdiction of Leasehold Valuation Tribunals.

The provisions in Part 2 of the Act are being introduced in a series of Commencement Orders. A Commencement Order is an Order by the appropriate Minister setting out the date or dates on which particular sections of the Act are to become operative. Regulations are also made which set out the details of a particular section, such as the Regulations amending s20 of the Landlord and Tenant Act 1985.

The first Commencement Order came into force immediately in July 2002 and brought the following measures into force:

- Amending the qualifying rules for collective enfranchisement, including
- Rights of access for valuation purposes, and
- Amending the treatment of marriage values
- Making the variation of leases easier in certain circumstances
- Allowing three party leases to use the right to seek an appointment of manager

The second Commencement Order brought into force the following provisions in England from 30 September 2003:

- The Right to Manage
- A widened definition of service charges to include improvements
- The right to challenge administration charges
- The right to demand information on buildings insurance policies
- A widened jurisdiction for Leasehold Valuation Tribunals

And from 31 October 2003, the amendments to s20 of the Landlord and Tenant Act 1985.

A third Commencement Order to be published in 2004 will bring the remaining sections of Part 2 of the Act into force, including forfeiture procedure changes, the requirement for notices for billing ground rent and service charges, the requirement for individual scheme bank accounts, a right to a regular statement of account, new provisions affecting insurance rights, and the rules for Right to Enfranchise companies.

Part 1 including the provisions for converting leasehold into commonhold will not come into force until later in 2004.

The table on pages 16-21 shows which landlords are affected by the amendments and new provisions of the Act.

■ The key changes introduced in the Commonhold and Leasehold Reform Act 2002

Service charges

The changes made by the 2002 Act are both detailed and far-reaching. Most are made through amendments to the Landlord and Tenant Acts of 1985 and 1987, and to the Housing Act 1996, although some changes are entirely new and originate in the 2002 Act. **They also apply to periodic tenants who pay variable service charges**.

Although the changes are fundamental, and the existing legislation is piecemeal, the 2002 Act has not set out to rationalise matters, so leasehold managers will still need to refer to the amendments to earlier Acts and to the 2002 Act.

To further complicate matters the changes are not detailed in the 2002 Act, which simply enables the detail to be contained in the Commencement Orders.

The main changes are:

- Expansion of the **definition of service charges** to encompass works of improvement
- **Revised procedures and financial limits for consulting leaseholders** about major works and improvements (Qualifying Works)
- A new **requirement to consult on service contracts of more than 12 months** duration (Qualifying Long Term Agreements)
- A new requirement for **regular statements of service charge accounts** within 6 months of the end of an accounting period. Previously a statement had to be provided only upon request, although local authorities and housing associations were already expected to do this under their respective regulation regimes, and most private sector managers already do so.

Contd. page 22…

Commonhold and Leasehold Reform Act 2002 Part 2 – leasehold reform provisions

	Generally will apply to:					Commencement Orders issued
	Local authority leaseholders	Charitable housing associations' leaseholders	Non-charitable housing associations' leaseholders	Shared ownership leaseholders	Private sector leaseholders	
Right to Manage *Chapter 1 - ss71-113* New Right to Manage, which will enable leaseholders to take over the management of their building without proving fault on the part of their landlord or needing to pay compensation	NO (LA tenants have separate right to manage which includes all tenants and long leaseholders)	YES	YES	NO	YES	**Com. Order 2** in August 03 implemented from 30 September 03
Collective Enfranchisement by leaseholders of flats *Chapter 2 - ss114-128* Collective enfranchisement made easier for leaseholders of flats – (amends Chap. 1 Part 1 Leasehold Reform, Housing and Urban Development Act 1993)	YES	NO	YES	NO Not until 100% of equity is purchased	YES	**Com. Order 1** July 2002 changed the valuation rules. Basic rules re. use of companies **Com. Order 3** expected mid-2004
New Leases for tenants of flats *Chapter 3 - ss129-136* Lease extensions and new longer leases made easier for leaseholders of flats (amends Chap. 2 Part 1 Leasehold Reform, Housing and Urban development Act 1993)	YES	NO	YES	NO	YES	**Com. Order 1** 26 July 02 Removes residence requirement & simplifies rules on qualifying leases, marriage value & Crown leaseholders

	Generally will apply to:					Commencement Orders issued
	Local authority leaseholders	Charitable housing associations' leaseholders	Non-charitable housing associations' leaseholders	Shared ownership leaseholders	Private sector leaseholders	
Enfranchisement of leasehold houses *Chapter 4 – ss137-149* Eases the ability of leaseholders to buy the freehold and obtain lease extensions – similar rights to those for flat leaseholders Special rules apply to leases of houses bought under the Right to Buy Some other exclusions including in rural locations (amends Leasehold Reform Act 1967 c.88)	YES	no	YES	no	YES	**Com. Order 1 26 July 02** Removes residence requirement & simplifies rules on qualifying leases, marriage value & Crown leaseholders. Abolishes low rent test. Excludes some business tenancies and some rural properties.
Service charges and administration charges *Chapter 5 – ss150-172 and Scheds. 9,10,11* Definition of service charge extended to include improvements and allow it to be extended further by regulation	YES	YES	YES	YES	YES	**Com. Order 1** introduces powers and confers power to make regulations
Chapter 5 s150 and Sched. 9 Service charge consultation requirements widened and revised	YES	YES	YES	YES	YES	**Com. Order 2** in August 03 implemented detailed requirements from 31 October 03
Major works prescribed amount to be increased and extended to long term contracts – *s151*	YES	YES	YES	YES	YES	

	Generally will apply to:					
	Local authority leaseholders	Charitable housing associations' leaseholders	Non-charitable housing associations' leaseholders	Shared ownership leaseholders	Private sector leaseholders	Commencement Orders issued
Service charges and administration charges – contd. Revised arrangements for accounting for leaseholders monies:	YES	YES	YES	YES	YES	**Com. Order 3** expected mid-2004
Leaseholders given right to an audited statement of account within 6 months of the end of the accounting period without need to request it.	YES	YES	YES	YES	YES	
In certain circumstances leaseholder can withhold payment of service charge	YES	YES	YES	YES	YES	
s152 Notice to accompany demands for service charges – s153	YES	YES	YES	YES	YES	**Com. Order 1 26 July 02** introduces powers and confers power to make regulations
Timescale to inspect receipts invoices reduced from 2 months to 21 days	YES	YES	YES	YES	YES	
Leaseholders can ask for copies of receipts/invoices to be sent to them for a fee s154	YES	YES	YES	YES	YES	**Com. Order 3** in mid-2004 will implement detailed requirements

	Generally will apply to:					
	Local authority leaseholders	Charitable housing associations' leaseholders	Non-charitable housing associations' leaseholders	Shared ownership leaseholders	Private sector leaseholders	Commencement Orders issued
Individual scheme bank accounts required s156	NO	NO	YES	YES	YES	
Notice of leaseholders' rights to accompany demands for service charges	YES	YES	YES	YES	YES	
Administration charges (eg charges for granting approvals) specifically made challengeable on grounds of reasonableness – s158 & Sched. 11	YES	YES	YES	YES	YES	Com. Order 2 August 2003 Implemented from 30 September 2003
Requirement that charges levied under estate management schemes are subject to a test of reasonableness determined by the LVT	YES	YES	YES	YES	YES	
Variation of leases Extended and clarified grounds for seeking lease variations – s162	YES	YES	YES	YES	YES	Com. Order 1 26 July 02
Insurance Changes to provisions relating to requests for insurance information	YES	YES	YES	YES	YES	Com. Order 2 August 2003

	Local authority leaseholders	Generally will apply to: Charitable housing associations' leaseholders	Non-charitable housing associations' leaseholders	Shared ownership leaseholders	Private sector leaseholders	Commencement Orders issued
New rights for leaseholders of houses with regard to insurers – ss164,165	YES	YES	YES	YES	YES	Com. Order 3 Expected mid-2004
Ground rent Requirement on landlords to give prescribed notice when demanding ground rent – s166	YES	YES	YES	YES	YES	Com. Order 3 Expected mid-2004
Forfeiture of leases of dwellings Protection against forfeiture increased – ss167-171	YES	YES	YES	YES	YES	Com. Order 3 Expected mid-2004
Crown application Extension of new and existing rights to Crown leaseholders – s172	N/A	N/A	N/A	N/A	YES	Com. Order 1 26 July 02
Leasehold Valuation Tribunals *Chapter 6 ss173-176* Extended jurisdiction of LVTs to hear any dispute over liability to pay service charges and the reasonableness of the works or charge	YES	YES	YES	YES	YES	Com. Order 2 in August 2003. Implemented September/ October 2003

	Local authority leaseholders	Charitable housing associations' leaseholders	Non-charitable housing associations' leaseholders	Shared ownership leaseholders	Private sector leaseholders	Commencement Orders issued
			Generally will apply to:			
Provisions in relation to constitution and procedures of LVTs	YES	YES	YES	YES	YES	
Permissions for appeals against LVT determinations to the Lands Tribunal	YES	YES	YES	YES	YES	
Implementation of recommendations of Financial and Policy Management Review in respect of LVTs	YES	YES	YES	YES	YES	

- Demands for service charges must always be accompanied by a **summary of the rights and obligations of the leaseholder in respect of service charges**, in a prescribed form. A leaseholder will be able to withhold payment if their landlord fails to comply.

- A new **requirement for service charge contributions to be held in a separate designated account**, available for inspection; failure to comply is a criminal offence. This does not however apply to local authorities and housing associations.

- The Act also introduces **controls on leases that provide for administration charges** that fall outside the definition of service charges in the lease. The Act lists the goods and services which can be separately charged for in this way.

- The **right to a summary of insurance cover and inspection of insurance documents** and to challenge the choice of insurer is strengthened, and leaseholders of houses are given the absolute right to insure the property themselves, no matter what the lease says.

How these changes operate, and how leasehold managers need to respond to them is set out in more detail in Chapters 5, 6 and 7 of this guide.

Extension of the jurisdiction of Leasehold Valuation Tribunals (LVTs)

Until the 2002 Act LVTs were only able to consider matters of 'reasonableness', which means – *is the charge reasonable, and is it reasonable for the work to be undertaken?* LVTs could not determine whether a charge was *payable* or not – ie *do the terms of the lease enable the landlord to make the charge?* Under the 2002 Act LVTs are empowered to interpret the service charge covenants in a lease and to determine any dispute as to the 'payability' of a service charge. The effect of this is also to give LVTs the power to determine counterclaims by the leaseholder and thus to decide whether the landlord is in breach of covenant.

LVTs are also given the power to vary lease terms and to control management and administration charges. LVTs will also be able to hear claims from landlords in respect of covenant breaches other than failure to pay charges; and to waive service charge consultation requirements and section 20 notices in certain circumstances.

Many commentators view this substantial development of the LVTs as the first steps to the creation of dedicated housing courts. There remain significant concerns over the absence of increased resources to enable LVTs to exercise these new powers and keep within reasonable timescales.

The Leasehold Valuation Tribunals (Procedure) (England) Regulations 2003 (SI No 2099) contain the new procedures for making an application to an LVT under the 2002 Act.

The work of Leasehold Valuation Tribunals and advice on how landlords should approach their dealings with them is dealt with in Chapter 11 of this guide.

Forfeiture

The Act has introduced restrictions on the commencement of forfeiture proceedings, including service of notices under section 146 of the Law of Property Act 1925, and sets limits on the level of debt below which proceedings cannot be commenced.

It will not be possible to use forfeiture for debts of less than a prescribed amount (currently proposed to be £350 unless the debt has been outstanding for more than a prescribed period, currently proposed to be 3 years).

It will not be possible to use forfeiture in respect of other breaches of covenant unless the leaseholder has admitted the breach, or a court or valuation tribunal has determined that a breach has occurred.

It is also proposed that the Commencement Order bringing these requirements into force (currently scheduled for mid 2004), will also include protection for vulnerable leaseholders who are unable to respond to proceedings.

The Right to Manage

This is the most radical of the leasehold reforms contained in the Act. Leaseholders will now be able to exercise their Right to Manage (RTM), even if the landlord or current manager is not at fault under the law or terms of the lease. It affects all landlords except local authorities, where a separate right to manage scheme for local authority tenants and leaseholders exists under the Housing Act 1985 and the Housing (Right to Manage) Regulations 1994 (SI 1994 No 627). The local authority scheme follows a completely different set of procedures and criteria.

The Right to Manage applies to eligible leaseholders in qualifying properties where not less than half the leaseholders participate in the RTM Company, and not less than two thirds of the flats are let on qualifying leases. The RTM does not apply to houses or bungalows.

Other non-qualifying properties are set out in Schedule 6 of the Act and include:

- Premises where any non-residential element exceeds 25% of the total internal floor area,
- Premises containing self-contained parts in freehold ownership, and
- Converted premises with no more than 4 flats, where one flat is occupied as the landlord's principal home or that of a member of their family.

Leaseholders will be required to form a Right to Manage company limited by guarantee, and will have to comply with company law in respect of filing returns, liability of directors and other matters. The company will need to serve notices on non-participating leaseholders inviting them to join. A notice must be served on the landlord who may serve a counter notice, only on very limited grounds, denying entitlement to the RTM, in which case a Leasehold Valuation Tribunal will have to make a determination.

Once the RTM Company is established, it takes over the management of the premises with no premium or compensation payable to the landlord.

The Commencement Order for this part of the Act took effect from 30 September 2003. The rules are contained in The Right to Manage (Prescribed Particulars and Forms (England) Regulations 2003 (SI No 1988) and model Memorandum and Articles for RTM Companies are provided in the RTM Companies (Memorandum and Articles of Association) (England) Regulations 2003 (SI No 2120).

The procedures under which the RTM can be exercised are complex and deal with matters such as absentee landlords who cannot be contacted for the service of notices. There will be a need for procedures for dealing with the collapse of a RTM company and measures to deal with existing management and maintenance contracts that the landlord may have entered into.

The current view is that such contracts are 'frustrated' under contract law as the landlord is no longer capable of fulfilling its part of the contract, but the implications of this are far reaching for both landlords and contractors, and may be the subject of further regulation.

As a matter of good practice any contract entered into which results in works or services being provided to a block that may be subject to the RTM, should include measures that allow for this eventuality.

Collective Enfranchisement and Right to Enfranchise (RTE) companies
The right to collective enfranchisement was introduced in the Leasehold Reform, Housing and Urban Development Act 1993. The 2002 Act relaxes the qualifying conditions and extends the range of property to which it can be applied.

The right is not available to shared ownership leaseholders until they have acquired a 100% equity interest, or to the leaseholders of charitable housing associations.

It is now no longer necessary for half the residents to have occupied their homes for the last 12 months, or for 3 years in the last 10, nor is it necessary for at least two thirds of the qualifying residents to join in the notice exercising the right – this has been reduced to "at least one half" of qualifying residents.

The Act requires that in every case except for cases dealt with in the paragraph below, the landlord's share of the marriage value is 50 per cent.

The Act also requires that, where the unexpired term of the existing lease exceeds eighty years, the marriage value shall be taken to be nil.

Property was excluded under the 1993 Act if 10% or more of the floor space was used for non-residential purposes. The new Act has increased this to 25%, which will bring significantly more mixed use buildings with shops or other commercial premises on part of the ground floor within the Right to Enfranchisement rules.

The detailed regulations including the prescribed forms, memorandum and articles, which were expected in the Second Commencement Order, have now been delayed and are unlikely to appear before mid 2004.

Enfranchisement (houses)

As with collective enfranchisement, the requirement that individual leaseholders seeking an extended long lease should satisfy a residence requirement is removed. Instead leaseholders simply have to have been a qualifying leaseholder for the previous two years before the exercise of the right to acquire an extended long lease.

❏ 2.5 The Companies Act 1985

Over half of private sector leasehold flats are owned and managed by the leaseholders themselves, or managed by an agent appointed by the leaseholders (Survey of English Housing 1998/99). The most common structure used is a flat management company, sometimes called a resident management company.

The prime purpose of limited companies is to limit the liabilities of the shareholders. In exchange for this limited liability, companies are required to make certain information about themselves available to the public. This information is filed at Companies House, and law governs the frequency and presentation of the information.

Flat management companies, although mostly formed for a different purpose, are governed by the same legislation – primarily, the Companies Act 1985. It does not allow flat management companies to be treated any differently to other companies.

Some limited companies do not have shares and are instead 'limited by guarantee'. If the company is limited by guarantee, it means that it has no shareholders, but has guarantors who have pledged to pay a (usually) nominal sum to the company if it is wound up. Right to Manage and Right to Enfranchise companies created under the Commonhold and Leasehold Reform Act 2002 will be companies limited by guarantee.

Failure to deliver company documents on time to Companies House is a criminal offence. A company could also be struck off the register and dissolved. In this case all assets (such as the freehold of the property if owned by the flat management company) would become 'bona vacantia'. This means they belong to the Crown. The company would then not be able to sell its freehold and may find that flats cannot be sold, without applying to the Courts to restore the company, which is an expensive exercise.

❏ 2.6 Supporting People

Supporting People is a national policy programme designed to assist people with support needs to live independent lives in suitable accommodation. The programme is underpinned by the Supporting People budget, which is administered by local authorities and their partners in the health and probation services.

From April 2003 the Supporting People Budget is being used to meet the costs of services required to support the individual, including those that may be provided by, or in conjunction with, the landlord. A key feature of the administration of the Supporting People budget is therefore the need to separate support costs from the costs of other services that the landlord may be providing.

In the case of leaseholders qualifying for assistance from the Supporting People Budget the information required to establish their housing related support costs has been tortuous to gather. The local authority Supporting People teams relied on the Pensions Service or Jobcentre Plus to provide them with details of the support charges awarded to individual qualifying leaseholders, but neither service holds sufficiently detailed information to separate support charges from service charges. The only way they have been able to do this is from the individual service charge statements that landlords have provided to their leaseholders.

The new Supporting People programme has most impact on leaseholders and managers of retirement housing, but also on the small number of leasehold supported housing schemes as well.

Key points about sheltered housing for sale and Supporting People

Leasehold schemes sit outside the Supporting People commissioning process, contract scheme review process and quality and monitoring process:

- There are no contracts with providers. The only contracts are with individual leaseholder claimants
- With respect to Supporting People, leasehold schemes are a payment process to the individual claimant, not a charging process
- There are no direct payments to providers
- The providers do not know which leaseholders are claiming income support.
- Most leaseholders are concerned that their financial circumstances are not revealed to their landlord, and their preference for confidentiality should be accepted and handled sensitively

---

Guarantees to leaseholders

Leaseholders have been given the same guarantees as for sheltered housing tenants:

- No existing residents will be 'reassessed' for their eligibility for leasehold provision of support since this is a contractual matter between leaseholder and landlord. Social services will not reassess for continuing residency or receipt of support services.

- Residents have a right to the level of support as outlined in their lease and will continue to receive that service.

- Access to leasehold provision should be based on older people's choices, including the choice to move away from their local area. It is not subject to any eligibility criteria.

Detailed guidance can be obtained from the ODPM Supporting People Team website and from the Association of Retirement Housing Managers (ARHM).

ARHM Good Practice Note on handling frailty in retirement leasehold schemes

ARHM publishes a guide that advises managers in relation to:

- Respecting the choice of residents
- Supporting the scheme manager
- Obtaining an assessment of a residents needs
- Building long-term relationships with social services
- How to respond to sudden changes in the condition of a resident
- Services available to residents in retirement housing
- Handling mental frailty
- Handling moves into residential care
- What to do if social services refuse access to residential care?
- Handling frailty of purchasers of retirement housing
- Dealing with requests to transfer the lease from the older resident to a younger family member

A list of useful contacts is also provided.

❑ 2.7 Codes of practice for leasehold management

There are two codes of good practice, both given statutory approval under s87 of the Leasehold Reform, Housing and Urban Development Act 1993. They are the *Code of Practice for Private Sheltered Housing* published by the Association of Retirement Housing Managers (ARHM) and the *Service Charge Residential Management Code* published by the Royal Institution of Chartered Surveyors (RICS).

Section 87 allows the Government to approve codes designed to promote desirable practices in relation to any matters concerned with the management of residential property.

Failure to comply with an approved code does not itself cause a landlord to commit an offence. However in any proceedings before a court or a tribunal an approved code is admissible in evidence, and any provision of an approved code which appears relevant to any court or tribunal will be taken into account in determining the case. There is particular reference to the codes in the grounds for the appointment of a manager under s24 of the Landlord and Tenant Act 1987.

Both codes are intended not simply as advice to managers and landlords, but also for leaseholders to use as consumer protection. Both codes provide a summary of relevant law and further assist leaseholders by stating good practice that leaseholders should be able to expect from their landlords or managing agents.

■ The Association of Retirement Housing Managers' Code
The Association of Retirement Housing Managers (ARHM) Code applies to private sheltered or retirement schemes only. The definition used is "leasehold residential properties which are specifically designed and designated for retired older people". In most cases this code also applies to the management of freehold bungalows for retired older people.

The Code was first approved in January 1996 and an addendum to incorporate the Housing Act 1996 was added in December 1996.

This Code may refer to *"private"* sheltered or retirement housing but it does apply to all landlords and managers in England and Wales, including housing associations and local authorities if they manage this type of scheme. It is recognised by the Housing Corporation in its bank of good practice.

The latest version of this Code which will incorporate the 2002 Act is in preparation and is expected to be approved in spring 2004.

■ The Royal Institution of Chartered Surveyors' Code
The Royal Institution of Chartered Surveyors' (RICS) Code applies to schemes where a variable service charge is payable, apart from private retirement schemes.

It was written for, and by, private sector landlords and managers in England and Wales, and it does *not* apply to local authorities or housing associations, although the Housing Corporation is currently considering whether it could apply to associations as good practice.

This Code was issued in February 1997 and a revised and updated version is in preparation to include the relevant provisions of the 2002 Act.

❏ 2.8 Regulation and inspection in the social sector

As well as complying with legislation and the terms of individual leases, local authority and housing association leasehold managers also need to take into account the requirements of their respective inspection regimes and of best value, and, for housing associations, the Housing Corporation's Regulatory Code and the new Charter for Housing Association Applicants and Residents .

Since April 2003 the Audit Commission has been responsible for inspections of both local authorities and housing associations. In both cases their approach to leasehold management, service charges and sales is likely to be more closely scrutinised in the future, and there are now specific characteristics of the landlord's approach that inspectors will expect to find in place. The level of importance that the Audit Commission will attach to the inspection of leasehold management services will depend upon the size of the landlord's leasehold stock, but when an inspection of "a whole housing service" is undertaken, inspectors will expect to find suitable leasehold management arrangements in place.

Private sector landlords and managing agents are not exposed to the same degree of regulation and inspection, but recent legislation has been enacted specifically to address what the Government has seen as widely varying standards of management.

Further legislation to provide improved voluntary controls by residential managers in the private sector, some form of tighter government regulation, or a licensing scheme for residential managers can be expected in the future, so it is in everyone's interests to ensure that high standards of residential management are applied throughout both the public and private sectors.

■ Housing Corporation regulation

Historically, the Housing Corporation's leasehold regulation has concentrated on shared ownership, but now there is much greater recognition of the range of management settings under which associations manage property.

The Housing Corporation now recognises that in practice associations have always had a small number of Right to Buy leaseholders and rather more leaseholders in specifically developed leasehold schemes for the elderly. As associations' property portfolios have diversified and expanded, and transfers of estates have taken place, so the numbers of Right to Buy leaseholders have also grown substantially.

Added to this have been the 100 or so large scale voluntary stock transfers that broadly mirror the mix of secure tenants and leaseholders of equivalent local authorities.

Current estimates of the numbers of housing associations leaseholders are:

- Shared ownership   75,000
- Leasehold Schemes for the Elderly   37,500
- Other leaseholders (mainly Right to Buy, but some Preserved Right to Buy, Right to Acquire and Voluntary Purchase Grant leaseholders)   40,000

Regulatory Code and Guidance

The new Regulatory Code and Guidance published in 2002 introduced a less prescriptive and more outcome based approach to the regulation of housing associations. This means that within the overall framework associations are free to develop their own approach to leasehold management as long as certain principles are evident within it.

The Housing Corporation expects associations to adopt an approach that:

- Is shaped around its customers
- Provides quality homes that meet people's needs
- Makes the best use of resources

and that the service is characterised by being:

- Accessible
- Responsive and informative
- Revised in response to customer feedback
- Inclusive and non-discriminatory
- Informed and forward looking
- Safe and secure

and achieves continuous improvement and provides value for money.

Performance indicators

There are currently no specific published performance indicators for leasehold management, but these are being developed for shared ownership as a first step.

Codes of guidance

The Corporation already expects the ARHM Code of Guidance mentioned earlier in this chapter to be followed by associations and is considering whether the new RICS Code of Guidance, currently in preparation, could become a standard with which associations might comply.

A Charter for Housing Association Applicants and Residents

From 1 September 2003 the new charter for housing association applicants and residents sets out what they can expect from their housing association landlords. It replaces the eight charters issued in 1998 and 1999.

Housing associations registered with the Housing Corporation must distribute the Charter to all existing residents including leaseholders and shared owners whose home has been provided with public funding, and to those applying to become a leaseholder or shared owner or tenant.

Associations should check that they are providing what the Charter says they *must* – ie because a right in law exists or because it is required under the regulatory code – or *should* which means the Corporation considers it to be good practice.

The Charter covers the following matters that are of relevance to leaseholders.

All leaseholders *must* be given:

- A copy of their lease
- Information on how the rent is set, levels of rent across all of the landlord's homes and the local area and about the landlord's performance in collecting the rent
- Information about the type of charges to be paid, what the costs are for and how they are set, and written notice must be given of any changes and increases to service charges
- Information about proposed improvements for which they will be required to pay
- Information and assistance about benefits if they have difficulty in paying rent or service charges
- The opportunity to participate in decision making and to contribute to how services are run and standards set

And all leaseholders *should* be given:

- A handbook or information about their landlord and its policies and practices
- Advice in respect of care and support services where appropriate

- Information about financial rights and responsibilities
- Information about their landlord's activities and what it is doing for the local community and how well it is performing

In addition associations are required to ensure that:
- Best value reviews take place
- Sinking funds are held in trust and the money used for the purpose specified in the lease
- If they own or manage leasehold schemes for older people, they have regard for the ARHM code of practice
- Services are shaped round customers' needs and that their views are sought and responded to
- They have an effective complaints and compensation policy
- Consultation on major works and long term plans for maintenance takes place in accordance with legislation
- That they consult leaseholders if they are considering changes to the arrangements for management or maintenance (including changing from a non-charitable to charitable association)

The leaseholders' guarantee issued in 1989 has been withdrawn for new leases, but some existing leases still refer to it, as do some LSVT guarantees to residents, so compliance with the leaseholders' guarantee will remain a contractual obligation for some associations.

Other matters
The Housing Corporation and the National Housing Federation are developing a standard form of leaseholders' survey for use by associations.

■ Central Government guidance
It is probably fair to say that at the time of writing this guide Government policy on residential leasehold management is at something of a crossroads.

The acknowledgement of weaknesses in the quality of leasehold management and the need to address these is constantly tempered by concern about the costs of any regulatory regime falling upon leaseholders.

Much of the detail of the operational effect of the Commonhold and Leasehold Reform Act has yet to become clear. A major consultation paper *Improving the Standard of Residential Leasehold Management* (April 2002) proposed a number of options for the introduction of licensing, regulation or a system of voluntary controls in the leasehold management sector, but the results of consultation have not yet led to any further proposals for legislative change.

❑ 2.9 Other sources of guidance for landlords and managers

There are two main trade bodies that represent landlords and managers as organisations in the private sector, the Association of Residential Managing Agents (ARMA) and the Association of Retirement Housing Managers (ARHM).

ARMA has over 120 corporate members, managing some 400,000 leasehold units. ARMA has a code of practice for its members that refers to contractual duties, financial duties and standards of services expected of its members. ARMA also publishes guidance notes for its members and a quarterly newsletter.

A growing number of housing associations have also affiliated to ARMA and follow its code of practice.

The **ARHM** was founded in June 1991 and has developed an important role in the management of retirement housing. The ARHM represents 53 organisations that, between them, manage some 79,000 out of the total 102,000 retirement properties in the UK.

The ARHM is a body which jointly represents the private sector and those registered social landlords who provide leasehold retirement housing. Over half of its members are housing associations.

The ARHM has published over 20 good practice notes for members on aspects of the management of retirement schemes.

■ The Leasehold Advisory Service (LEASE)

The Leasehold Advisory Service (LEASE) is a free source of specialist advice on all aspects and issues relating to residential leasehold property and is sponsored by the ODPM. It is available to leaseholders and also to all landlords and managers. It publishes a wide range of advice materials including information on collective enfranchisement for flats, lease extension for flats and enfranchisement for leasehold houses. Its website also provides access to all the decisions and determinations of Leasehold Valuation Tribunals.

■ The Institute of Residential Property Managers (IRPM)

The IRPM was launched in 2002 and is a professional body for individuals who work in leasehold management. Its aim is to develop a professional qualification and exams for leasehold managers. It is working with the Chartered Institute of Housing to develop a syllabus for an advanced professional qualification, the first part of which became available in 2002.

■ Advice Information and Mediation Service (AIMS)

AIMS is an impartial service for landlords, managers and leaseholders of private retirement housing, including schemes owned or managed by housing associations.

In 2002 AIMS received an Innovation and Good Practice Grant from the Housing Corporation to carry out specific project work for three years related to how the Right To Manage (RTM) might affect landlords, managers and residents in private retirement housing. It will provide an impartial and independent advice and dispute resolution service specifically targeted to address the issues of RTM for the private retirement sector. AIMS has produced a detailed information sheet on RTM which is available free of charge.

■ The Housing Ombudsman Service (incorporating the Independent Housing Ombudsman Scheme) and the Local Government Ombudsman

Under the Housing Act 1996, all registered social landlords in England must be members of the Independent Housing Ombudsman Scheme (IHOS). Other landlords including private landlords, subsidiaries of social landlords, and other independent bodies who provide housing services, may join on a voluntary basis. Complaints about local authorities are dealt with by the Local Government Ombudsman.

IHOS will take up complaints from leaseholders only where the internal complaints procedures of the organisation have been fully exhausted. The Local Government Ombudsman operates on a broadly similar basis and is able to take complaints directly from leaseholders or by referral from a member of the local authority.

Both bodies publish digests of cases that are useful guides for both landlords and residents, and can act as indicators of trends in the quality of leasehold management.

❑ 2.10 Further reading on the legal and regulatory framework for leasehold management

The Housing Corporation (HC) – Regulatory Code and Guidance, circulars, information, inspection reports
www.housingcorp.gov.uk

The Audit Commission – Best value review inspection reports and other information
www.audit-commission.gov.uk

Commonhold and Leasehold Reform Act 2002
www.legislation.hmso.gov.uk/acts/acts2002/20020015.htm

Association of Retirement Housing Managers (1996 – revised edition due spring 2004) *Code of Practice for Private Sheltered Housing*   ISBN 0 952699 0 2
Statutory approval given under s87 Leasehold Reform, Housing and Urban Development Act 1993

Royal Institution of Chartered Surveyors (1997 – revised edition in progress) *Service Charge Residential Management Code* ISBN 0 85406 643 8
Statutory approval given under s87 Leasehold Reform, Housing and Urban Development Act 1993

The Leasehold Advisory Service – LEASE – an independent advice agency funded by government grant – various information and guidance available including details of LVT decisions
www.lease-advice.org

The Association of Residential Managing Agents (ARMA) has a code of practice and provides information and guidance for its members
www.arma.org.uk

AIMS – advice and mediation service for people living in and managing sheltered housing – rented and leaseholders – part of Age Concern
www.ageconcern.org.uk

The Institute of Residential Property Managers – professional body for those who work in leasehold property management
www.irpm.org.uk

Housing Corporation *Charter for Housing Association Applicants and Residents*

Office of the Deputy Prime Minister (ODPM) website for news and downloadable documents regarding leasehold issues
www.housing.odpm.gov.uk/information/leaseholdreform

Residential Property Tribunal Service (RPTS)
www.rpts.gov.uk

ODPM Supporting People Team – Regularly updated site on the progress of the Supporting People Programme
www.spkweb.org.uk

CHAPTER 3

THE IMPORTANCE OF THE LEASE

This chapter explains the features of a typical lease and how leases should be used in practice.

It sets out some basic principles for the drafting and review of leases and explains breaches of lease provisions and how to vary a lease.

❏ 3.1 Introduction

■ What is a lease?

The lease is a binding contract that sets out the terms on which the landlord allows the leaseholder to occupy the property described in the lease. The lease governs the relationship between the landlord and the leaseholder setting out their respective rights and obligations. It is enforceable in law – the parties to it cannot simply walk away from a lease or decide unilaterally to act outside the terms of it. However, variation *is* possible by agreement of *all* the parties to the lease and in certain circumstances by application to the LVT.

Unfortunately, leases are often lengthy, complicated and poorly drafted. Leaseholders' understanding of their leases is generally weak, and managers may not even have access to leases for the properties they manage, never mind a proper understanding of them.

As a general principle, the lease should be regarded as the main determining factor in relation to the way in which a property is managed and maintained. It is essential that leasehold managers have a detailed understanding of the provisions of all the leases in use by the landlord and access both to plain English summaries of those provisions and to the lease itself.

■ Types of lease

Subject to overriding legal requirements, it is up to the landlord and leaseholder to agree the terms of the lease. There is no standard form of lease; however, there are certain matters that will be contained in almost all leases, and the Law Society produces model leases for various types of tenancy.

For housing associations, the Housing Corporation provides sample leases for shared ownership and retirement housing which associations can use or adapt.

Leases for properties sold under the Right to Buy, either by local authorities or non-charitable housing associations, must comply with Schedule 6 of the 1985 Housing Act in outline, though they vary widely in practice.

Leases for Right to Acquire sales follow the Right to Buy format, but there is no model document.

Each landlord's solicitor will have the responsibility for drawing up leases. Clearly, drafting a good lease and ensuring some consistency amongst leases used is a crucial step towards good leasehold management. One indication of the quality of leases will be their success in reducing queries, disputes and ultimately, litigation.

❑ 3.2 The main features of a lease

■ Typical structure

A typical lease will be structured as follows:

- Land Registry details including the title number of the land out of which the lease is granted
- Details of the parties to the lease
- Definitions of terms used in the lease
- The date of the lease and how long it will run for ("the term")
- A definition of the area and elements of the dwelling which are granted to the leaseholder and those other elements of the building/estate over which rights are/may be granted together with a plan marked up with the information
- The basic terms of the agreement including the landlords' obligations and the leaseholders' obligations (landlords' and leaseholders' covenants)
- These covenants relate to what items of expenditure can be included by the landlord in a service charge and all arrangements relating to calculation of service charges for the block/building and estate, as well as for the payment of charges and ground rent

■ Schedules to the lease

There will often be schedules which describe the rights the landlord and the leaseholder have over each other's property – usually:

- A schedule detailing the rights the leaseholder has over land which is not included in their lease
- A schedule describing the rights the landlord has retained over the property in the lease
- A schedule describing the obligations of the leaseholder
- A schedule describing the obligations of the landlord
- A schedule detailing the regulations that the leaseholder agrees to adhere to
- A schedule detailing the items of expenditure to be included in the estate/block service charges

■ Other aspects of a lease

Leases will also specify a range of other matters. These will include, but not be limited to:

- The purchase price or 'premium'
- With Right to Buy sales, details of repayment of discounts
- With shared ownership, details of rent and rent increases and future staircasing
- Arrangements for subletting or assigning the lease

Many landlords will have a number of different leases issued at different times and in respect of different categories of leasehold. Even where there are standard model leases available it is common to find several variations to them that have evolved over a period of time.

While it is desirable for landlords to try and standardise the main clauses used in newly drafted leases, it will still be essential for staff to refer to individual leases before responding to queries. Purchasers' solicitors may occasionally seek changes to the lease offered, but these should be resisted wherever possible, and the landlord's solicitors and managing agents should be made aware that they have no authority to agree changes to the standard lease without reference to the landlord.

❑ 3.3 Using the lease

The lease sets the framework for management of the property. It is used to:

- check where responsibility lies – for example in respect of types of repair
- check if there is provision in the lease to do something – for example to charge for a specific service or supply
- ensure that the landlord is meeting its obligations to the leaseholder

Bromford Housing Group places a lease summary on the front of each scheme service charge file. A description can be found in Chapter 5.8 of this guide.

When using the lease it is important to remember that the rights and obligations it contains can be overridden by legislation. As an example, the terms of some leases may state only what the service charge includes and how it is to be paid. The Landlord and Tenant Acts extend this to require that service charge costs must be reasonably incurred and the services must be to a reasonable standard.

Where a lease is not explicit or there is a conflict between legislation and the lease then the requirements of legislation must be followed.

The landlord is obliged to provide the services specified in the lease unless there is a provision in the lease to vary them. This means that before any decision is taken to change the services provided to a building or estate where there are leaseholders, the provisions of the lease should be checked and taken into account.

The landlord can only recover the cost of services if there is a provision to do so in the lease. For example if the landlord mistakenly carried out a repair that was the obligation of the leaseholder, the cost of this could not be recovered from the leaseholder as there will be no provision for this in the lease. If additional services are provided which are not specified in the lease then the costs may not be recoverable.

If the form of the service charge calculation is specified in the lease with the timescales for payment, then these timescales must be followed, but different methods of payment which are intended to offer easier terms, such as direct debit, can be introduced later without varying the lease. This may amount to a technical breach of the lease terms, but it is unlikely that such a benefit, if offered to all leaseholders, would provide adequate cause for action by a disgruntled leaseholder.

Using the lease: good practice principles

- A copy of the lease should be placed on the management file of each leasehold property, or if more practicable, a note of the location of an exact copy of the lease.
- All staff who will need to consult leases should have ready access to them at their place of work

→

- Summaries of leases produced in plain English by solicitors can be very helpful to leaseholders, potential purchasers and staff, and can be used as a focus for training
- All staff involved in any aspect of leasehold management should receive training about leases.
- Leases should be referred to regularly as working documents, for example:
  - to ensure that all the landlord's obligations to the leaseholder are being met
  - to ensure that there is a contractual basis for action taken by the landlord, for example to charge for certain items
  - to determine who has responsibility for items of repair
  - to check whether and what action can be taken against a leaseholder, for example in respect of breach of the terms of the lease
- At least one person or section within an organisation should be familiar with the terms of the leases in use
- That person should be able to provide basic advice on leases to front line staff, and be able to decide in what circumstances external legal advice will be required

In some local authorities the leasehold management task is made more difficult because leases are retained in the legal department for fear that they will be wrongly interpreted by housing staff. This practice should be countered by training and support so that staff are clear as to when and on what issues they will need to seek legal advice and guidance. It is essential that leasehold managers and agents have access to the leases for property they manage, and that they refer only to the original leases or certified copies.

■ Drafting and reviewing leases

A lease should be clear and comprehensive, and the respective obligations of landlord and leaseholder easily understood. The terminology used should be clear and unambiguous.

A lease should accurately reflect the intentions and practices of the landlord and as far as possible anticipate future situations that may arise with regard to the property.

The form of lease should not rely on matters that are likely to change within a short time span, for example specific indices or cost allowances, unless provision is made for what happens when they are no longer relevant.

The lease should be reviewed periodically in the light of experience and legislative changes, and staff involved in managing the property should be involved in the review and any redrafting of master leases.

Where a new scheme is being developed there will be an opportunity to review the form of lease being used.

❏ 3.4 Varying the terms of existing leases

■ The need to vary leases

There are a number of reasons why landlords will wish to vary existing leases, but it is never an easy option and there will be very few cases where the cost in time and resources of seeking a variation will outweigh the possible benefits.

Both local authorities and housing associations are faced with managing leasehold properties occupied under a variety of different leases. In the case of local authorities there will be pre and post 1987 leases (following the changes introduced by the Housing and Planning Act 1986) and voluntary sales leases. Housing associations may hold leases entered into by a previous landlord in either the public or private sectors.

Both local authorities and associations may hold leases that were drawn up at a time before the demands of leasehold management were fully appreciated or at a time when the financial consequences of managing leasehold properties were different.

As a result, many landlords have to consider varying the terms of existing leases, often with the aim of restricting the numbers of different leases in operation.

■ Varying lease terms by agreement

The terms of leases can be varied only by specific agreement between all the parties to the lease and, where appropriate, their mortgagees, or through an order by a Leasehold Valuation Tribunal. Landlords have rarely found it possible to reconcile the interests of all leaseholders. For example it is common to find one or two lessees who will take a different view from the others about the need for a new or different level of service, often for financial reasons.

Where it can be achieved by agreement, it is desirable for a deed of variation to be drawn up and signed by both parties. This can be straightforward in the case of an individual leaseholder, but more commonly the landlord is faced with the need to vary several leases and to obtain the consent of several mortgagees as well.

■ Varying lease terms by application to the LVT

The Landlord and Tenant Act 1987 provides that "any party to a long lease of a flat may make an application to the Court for an Order varying the lease in such manner as is specified in the application".

Under s163 of the Commonhold and Leasehold Reform Act 2002 this jurisdiction was transferred on 30 September 2003 to Leasehold Valuation Tribunals, and the grounds on which a lease may be varied are extended with provision made to further extend them by regulation.

Section 35 of the 1987 Act allows such applications to be made on the grounds that the existing terms are defective. This covers such matters as terms that effectively prevent the proper maintenance or upkeep of the building, or lead to unsatisfactory conditions of occupation, or prevent proper recovery of service charges.

The purpose is to enable leases to be 'modernised' to allow for circumstances that may not have been envisaged when the lease was first drawn up.

Section 37 provides for an application to vary two or more leases where there is general agreement about the variation. General agreement in this instance means at least 75% of the parties concerned where more than eight leases are involved, providing that not more than 10% of the parties actively object; or in the case of eight or fewer leases, where all but one party agrees. The landlord is a party to the lease and therefore is counted as one of the "parties concerned". The leases involved do not have to be identical, nor do they have to be in respect of dwellings in the same block.

If all parties agree on the application to the LVT the process can still take up to six months, but often there are objections, and in many cases the leaseholder's mortgagees will need to be served with notice of the application as well. This can lead to much longer and potentially costly proceedings to bring about the variation.

Where the property is specifically securing a loan, the landlord's lender will also need to be involved.

■ Varying leases for some leaseholders and not others

As an alternative the landlord can agree to vary the leases of those leaseholders who are in agreement and to replace or vary the remainder when the opportunity arises.

Obviously the nature of the proposed variation will govern the decision as to whether this is a realistic approach or whether it will lead to inequitable treatment of leaseholders.

Management difficulties can arise where new leases and old leases are operating together in the same block. However, remedying the problems is not always easy.

Introducing a covenant that restricts a new resident in ways that an existing resident is not restricted may be perfectly legal, but may lead to ill feeling that spills over into neighbour disputes. Similarly the landlord's need to recover costs of services that were not relevant when the first leases were drawn up may lead to apparently inequitable service charges when they are introduced into new leases.

Some leases expressly require the landlord to continue using the same lease in future sales within a defined group of homes, which makes it extremely difficult to bring about changes unless *all* leaseholders are in agreement.

This means weighing up the pros and cons of amending leases very carefully, with the involvement of managers and residents as well as lawyers and accountants.

❏ 3.5 Breaches of lease terms

If either the landlord or the leaseholder do not keep to the terms of the lease this is known as a breach of the covenant. Various legal remedies are available to make the parties to the lease conform to its terms or 'remedy' the breach. These include:

- Seeking an injunction to prevent the actions being taken which breach the lease
- Seeking an order of specific performance to compel an obligation to be carried out

In some circumstances, it may be possible to take an action for damages to compensate for the breach.

To deal with serious persistent breaches by the leaseholder the lease will include a clause that allows a right of re-entry to the property – a process known as forfeiture. Forfeiture is enforced by the landlord serving the appropriate notice on the leaseholder and then seeking an order for possession of the property through the courts. The courts have considerable discretion on whether to grant possession and this remedy is suitable only for the most serious cases. See Chapter 8.1 on Forfeiture.

❑ 3.6 Unfair terms in leases

The Unfair Terms in Contracts Regulations 1999 state that all tenancy agreements, including long leases, should not have unfair terms in them. The regulations apply to all leases granted since 1 July 1995.

Unfair terms are those made by the landlord in a standard contract, which give the landlord too much advantage over the leaseholder. Landlords drafting leases have a responsibility to make sure they do not contain any unfair terms.

Guidance issued by the Office of Fair Trading provides some examples of what may be considered unfair terms relevant to leases:

- Terms that bind leaseholders to accept rules and regulations that are not part of the lease or can be made after the lease is signed.
- A power for the landlord to make rules binding leaseholders is likely to be considered unfair if it gives a broad discretion.
- Forfeiture clauses need to acknowledge the leaseholder's legal rights at least in general terms. Terms that do not make clear that the landlord cannot evict without a court order may be open to objection.
- An absolute ban or excessive discretion to refuse consent upon assignment or subletting may be unfair.

For further information see Office of Fair Trading publication listed below.

❑ 3.7 Further reading on leases

Office of Fair Trading – *Guidance on unfair terms in tenancy agreements* ref OFT356 November 2001. See www.oft.gov.uk or obtain free of charge from 0870 6060321.

The Association of Residential Managing Agents (ARMA) has a code of practice and provides information and guidance for its members
www.arma.org.uk

The Association of Retirement Housing Managers (ARHM) – for Code of Practice, revised edition due spring 2004, also good practice notes for members
www.arhm.org

The Leasehold Advisory Service – LEASE – an independent advice agency funded by government grant – various information and guidance available including details of LVT decisions
www.lease-advice.org.uk

The Housing Corporation *Circular F2 68/89* introduced model shared ownership leases
www.housingcorp.gov.uk

Right to Buy leases – follow provisions specified in Schedule 6 Housing Act 1985

A-Z Guide for Legal Phrases – guidance being regularly updated – copyright by Plain English Campaign
www.plainenglish.co.uk

The Law Society – Model leases

CHAPTER 4

SALES AND SECTION 125 NOTICES

This chapter explains the general legal framework within which all landlords need to undertake sales. The very specific legislation and regulations concerning Right to Buy, Right to Acquire and shared ownership sales is already covered in other publications recommended at the end of the chapter.

However, readers' attention is drawn to the service of section 125 notices under the Housing Act 1985, as this fundamentally affects the landlord's ability to levy service charges following the sale.

❑ 4.1 The legislative framework for sales and marketing

All developers of leasehold homes have to operate their sales and marketing within the framework of consumer protection law. In addition local authorities and housing associations administering the Right to Buy and shared ownership schemes need to observe the requirements of the Housing Acts.

❑ 4.2 Legal requirements affecting all landlords

■ Property Misdescriptions Act 1991

Under this Act it is a criminal offence to make misleading or false statements about a prescribed matter when marketing a property for sale. The prescribed matters are set out in the Act and these cover all aspects about a property such as location, facilities and the level of service charges. All landlords' sales and resales activities are covered by the Act.

Local Trading Standards Officers are responsible for enforcing the provisions of the Act and they can instigate a prosecution without receiving a complaint from a member of the public. On conviction for an offence a fine is imposed. Both individuals and organisations can be liable under the Act.

The key points to note are:
- The Act covers any kind of promotion including:
  - written particulars in brochures, photographs, plans, architects' impressions, show houses, displays, adverts, posters, letters
  - meetings, discussions or telephone conversations with potential buyers
- A false or misleading statement is:
  - one which is false to a material degree
  - one that is misleading to a reasonable person
- It is not only misleading statements that cause an offence to be committed – misleading by omission is also an offence – and any disclaimers must be brought to the attention of the buyer, for example, that a location map is indicative or not to scale. Blanket disclaimers are not permitted under the Act.

To make certain they comply with the Act, landlords need to ensure that staff and external consultants, for example brochure writers, are aware of the Act. There should be systems and procedures in place to check all advertising and publicity materials and communications.

■ Financial Services and Markets Act 2000

This Act replaces the Financial Services Act 1986 which was introduced to provide protection for customers of investment businesses, which give advice on and arrange investments. The Act provides a new framework for the regulation of financial services and may affect housing associations that give advice in relation to mortgages.

Under the Act, anyone who carries out a "regulated activity" which includes providing investment advice or selling investment products must be authorised to do so or be exempt. It is a criminal offence to carry out these activities without being authorised or exempt. Obtaining authorisation is lengthy and associations are recommended to ensure they do not give investment advice and are not seen to be arranging investments. To avoid breaching this Act, landlords should not recommend a particular lender or a specific type of mortgage or assist buyers in completing or sending off forms for mortgages, endowment policies or other products.

Within the terms of the Act, landlords can:
- Give general advice about how mortgage finance works, as this is not covered by the Act. However it is recommended that this is only done by properly trained staff as the penalties for getting it wrong are severe.
- Give potential buyers introductions to independent financial advisors
- Provide a list of lenders which are known to give mortgages on shared ownership homes; it is recommended that the list is as long as possible
- Passively display leaflets, brochures etc, from different lenders in a reception or show home

Readers should note that the FSA will be regulating mortgages from October 2004.

■ Consumer Credit Act 1974

This Act provides that anyone carrying out certain activities in relation to credit or hiring must have a consumer credit licence. Any landlord wishing to recommend buyers to take advice from an independent financial intermediary or wishing to collect reservation deposits from buyers will need a consumer credit licence.

Any deposits taken should always be kept in separate client's accounts and should earn interest.

The licence is supplied by the Office of Fair Trading, lasts for five years and is relatively inexpensive. Many registered social landlords carrying out shared ownership have these licences.

■ Estate Agents Act 1979

This applies to landlords when carrying out resales activity. The initial sale of shared ownership homes does not fall within the definition of estate agency work for the purposes of this Act.

The Act provides that deposits given to estate agents are held on trust by the agent and should be held in a separate client account. There are also provisions relating to the details that an agent should give about his charges, and to the disclosure of any personal interest he has in property he is dealing with.

Unfit persons can be banned from carrying on estate agency work on the grounds of offences involving fraud, dishonesty, or violence; commission of offences under the Act; failing to comply with certain obligations under the Act, or discriminating in the course of estate agency work.

❏ 4.3 The various right to purchase schemes in the social housing sector

■ Right to Buy (RTB)

The 1980 Housing Act gave secure tenants of specific landlords the right to purchase their home at a price discounted in proportion to their length of residence as a public sector tenant – the Right to Buy (RTB). The provisions relating to the RTB are now found in Part V of the Housing Act 1985.

■ The Preserved Right to Buy (PRTB)

The Preserved Right to Buy (PRTB) originates in ss171 A–H of the Housing Act 1985, which defines circumstances in which the RTB for secure tenants, is *preserved* when there is a transfer of ownership to another landlord. To have the PRTB the conditions for a RTB must have been met prior to the transfer. Its operation is currently governed by the Housing (Preservation of the Right to Buy) Regulations 1993 and the Housing (Preservation of the Right to Buy) Amendment Regulations 1999.

■ The Right to Acquire (RTA)

The Right to Acquire (RTA) was introduced in ss16 and 17 of the Housing Act 1996 to enable the tenants of registered social landlords to purchase their homes. It only applies to dwellings built or acquired since 1 April 1997. Its operation is currently governed by:

- The Housing (Right to Acquire) Regulations 1997 (SI No 619)
- The Housing (Right to Acquire) (Discount) Order 2002 – (SI No 1091)
- The Housing (Right to Acquire or Enfranchise) (Designated Rural Areas) Order 1997 (SI Nos 622 to 625)
- Housing (Right to Acquire or Enfranchise) (Designated Rural Areas) Order 1999 (SI No 1307)

■ Voluntary Purchase Grant sales

The Voluntary Purchase Grant scheme was introduced in April 1996 and enables RSLs to dispose of homes to sitting tenants who do not have the Right to Acquire, as the homes they occupy were provided before 1 April 1997. A relatively small number of leaseholds will have been created under this scheme.

■ Conduct of right to purchase schemes sales

The statutory procedure requires the use of specific forms for the RTB and RTA and although the forms themselves are not specified for the PRTB, the information requirements make it safer and easier to use the specified forms for the RTB when processing sales under the PRTB.

❏ 4.4 Shared ownership sales – mainly housing associations

Shared ownership was introduced in 1980 and is governed under Part V of the Housing Act 1985. Prior to 1989 the Housing Corporation issued various model leases, but now is not prescriptive about leases, provided certain fundamental clauses are included.

Shared ownership sales take place against a background of vigorous marketing to minimise sales periods. It is important to remember that the long term relationship with the shared ownership leaseholder will be influenced by their experience during that sales period.

❏ 4.5 Sales of leasehold homes for the elderly

Homes within leasehold schemes for the elderly are sometimes sold outright and sometimes on the basis of a percentage share. This includes shared ownership for the elderly. Most schemes have an on site resident manager (warden) with a warden call system.

❏ 4.6 Administration of sales

■ Common problems with the sales process

The two most common problems are:

- Inadequate information provision to prospective leaseholders about their obligations and the terms of the lease resulting in a range of management difficulties at a later date
- The difficulty of assessing future service charge and major works costs due to poor information availability

■ The administration of the sales process

Many of the problems associated with the management of leasehold property stem either directly or indirectly from the pre-sales period. This is because pre-sales has often been seen as a process which is an end in itself, rather than the period for planning and setting the framework for future management of leasehold properties.

It is therefore worth ensuring that the management and administration of the sales process is properly resourced, continually reviewed and recognised as a long term corporate responsibility with significant financial and legal implications.

■ Providing information to prospective leaseholders

Both the Housing Corporation and the Government provide guidance on the type of information that should be given to prospective leaseholders by social landlords. There is an enormous difference between the information needs of sitting tenants purchasing the homes they live in and buyers of shared ownership and leasehold retirement housing.

For new leasehold sales under the Right to Buy and the Right to Acquire, there is a clear opportunity to improve the amount and type of information provided with the later impact of reduced management difficulties.

Leaflets written in plain English summarising rights and responsibilities are recommended and consideration should be given to carrying out interviews to go through this information in detail. Housing associations undertaking shared ownership sales have in some cases developed good practice which can be adapted in relation to Right to Buy or Right to Acquire sales.

The ARHM Code of Practice is very specific about the information to be given to purchasers and requires a handbook or purchasers information pack containing prescribed information to be given to the purchaser or their solicitor.

LEASE produces a booklet *Living in Leasehold* that gives a general introduction for purchasers.

■ Co-ordinating the sales process

A senior person should be nominated to co-ordinate the sales particularly during the initial stages of setting up a framework, developing legal documentation and setting up records and policies and procedures.

❏ 4.7 Section 125 notices

Whilst this guide does not deal with the Right to Buy sales process, the service of s125 offer notices has implications for future service charging and leasehold management.

When a tenant exercises their RTB, PRTB or RTA, s125 of the Housing Act 1985 requires the landlord to serve a notice giving them information about the terms of the proposed sale. This includes the following information about service charges:
- A description of the services for which charges will be made and an estimate of the average annual amount, at current prices, of those charges by head of charge
- Details of any known structural defects
- For itemised repairs, an estimate of the cost of each item and the likely contribution required from the leaseholder plus the total cost of all the items and all of the leaseholder's contributions. Repairs include works required to make good structural defects
- For non-itemised repairs, an estimate of the average annual amount, at current prices, likely to be required from the leaseholder
- An itemised list of improvements with an estimate of the cost of each item and the likely contribution required from the leaseholder for each, plus the total cost of all the items and all of the leaseholder's contributions

All these figures must be given for the reference period of 5 years. The period will generally be 5 years from a date, not later than 6 months after the service of the s125 notice, specified by the landlord as being the date by which it considers the sale will have taken place.

The initial period of a Right to Buy lease is the 5 year period starting from the date of completion of the sale. As the reference period is basically an estimate of the dates of the initial period, they will often coincide.

During the initial period the landlord's ability to recover service charges for repairs and improvements will be limited to those items included in the s125 notice and only up to the amount specified, plus an allowance for inflation.

A model s125 notice for use under the Right to Buy is provided on the following pages. Notices under the Right to Acquire are similar, but should not make reference to Rent to Mortgage which does not apply to RTA sales.

For sales under the Right to Acquire landlords should also refer to the Housing (Right to Acquire) Regulations 1997 (SI No 619).

Model documents for section 125 notices

RIGHT TO BUY UNDER THE HOUSING ACTS

NOTICE OF PURCHASE PRICE AND OTHER MATTERS

Enclosed are documents relevant to the proposed purchase of your home. They are:

1 **s125 Offer Notice**
This gives details of the market value, the discount you are entitled to, and the purchase price of your home. Details of the likely service charges are also shown, along with a notification of any structural defects known to the landlord that affect the dwelling.

2 **Draft Transfer/Lease**
These documents contain all the rules and obligations that you must abide by once you have purchased. The landlord will remain responsible for various services such as grounds maintenance, and the lease will describe what proportion of the costs you will be required to pay towards this.

3 **Site Plan**
This will be included in the transfer or lease and shows the areas that the landlord is responsible for maintaining. If you have a garden, "T" marks on the boundaries will indicate which fences you will be responsible for maintaining. The land you are purchasing will be indicated as described in the transfer/lease.

You must inform us *within 12 weeks* in writing whether

    a)   You wish to proceed with the purchase on Right to Buy terms

    b)   You wish to withdraw your application.

On receipt of the offer notice you may serve notice (Form RTB3) claiming the right to purchase on Rent to Mortgage terms (see additional notes and statement of relevant amounts).

If you decide to proceed, you will also need to contact a solicitor or licensed conveyancer and arrange the finance for your purchase with a bank or building society, but if you need any general advice, please contact me at the above address or telephone number.

Yours sincerely

Leasehold Manager

RIGHT TO BUY

Landlord's Offer Notice under s125 of the Housing Act 1985 (as amended by the Housing Planning Act 1986)

To: ……………………………………….........................

It has been established that you have the Right to Buy from (Landlord's Name) a lease for ……. years of the flat known as:
…………………………………..
…………………………………..
…………………………………..

The price at which in the landlord's opinion, you are entitled to make this purchase is £…………….. This price has been arrived at as follows:

Market Value at ……………….. ……………. (Date of the service by the Applicant of RTB/RTA 1)
Less discount of …………….

The discount has been calculated on the basis that the total period which may be taken into account for discount is ………………….. years.

The following improvements which you have carried out have been disregarded in arriving at the market value shown above.
……………………………………………………………………………………………….................
……………………………………………………………………………………………….................
……………………………………………………………………………………………….................
……………………………………………………………………………………………….................
……………………………………………………………………………………………….................

No structural survey has been made in connection with this valuation, nor have the services been tested, however the following structural defects are known to exist:
……………………………………………………………………………………………….................
……………………………………………………………………………………………….................
……………………………………………………………………………………………….................
……………………………………………………………………………………………….................
……………………………………………………………………………………………….................

You are advised to seek independent advice on the condition of the property.

Signed: …………….……………………………………………… Date: ………………
Sales Officer

ESTIMATED SERVICE CHARGES

As a leaseholder, you will be responsible for paying service charges. The following tables set out our estimates of the amount of service charges that you will have to pay.

The estimates are set out in the manner required by law. You will see that they cover both the costs of services that we will provide regularly each year and the costs of works that will be needed occasionally - such as external redecoration, or which are known to be required on a one-off basis.

Whilst we will be pleased to discuss these estimates with you, it is recommended that you also seek independent advice on any matters that may be of concern to you.

	Average annual amount
1. Estimated cost of day to day services	
Grounds maintenance	....
Communal lighting	....
Cleaning and caretaking	....
Lifts	....
Entry phone and concierge services	....
Sinking fund contribution	....
Management fee	....
Total estimated cost of day to day services	....
2. Estimated cost of day to day repairs and maintenance	
Unitemised works	....
Management fee	....
Total estimated cost of repairs & maintenance	....
3. Buildings Insurance	....

	Overall cost of works	Your contribution
4. Estimated cost of itemised works		
External redecorations (including communal areas)	....	....
Window replacement	....	....
Roof renewal	....	....
Other (define here)	....	....
	....	....
	....	....
Total estimated cost of itemised repairs	....	....

Important Notes

The above figures are estimates only and are given for guidance. The items included in sections 1 and 2 are likely to vary from year to year.

However, in the first 5 years we will only be able to recover services charges for the unitemised works shown in section 2, up to the amount stated, plus an allowance for inflation. Similarly, we will only be able to recover service charges for the itemised works shown in section 4 up to the amount stated, plus an allowance for inflation, and in respect of the items described.

NOTES RELATING TO THE INFORMATION PROVIDED IN THIS NOTICE UNDER SECTION 125 OF THE HOUSING ACT 1985

1. The discount to which you are entitled has been calculated in accordance with s129 of the Housing Act 1985.

2. You have a right under s128 of the Housing Act, to require that the valuation be determined or redetermined by the District Valuer, but you must give the landlord written notice within 3 months of the service of this Notice, if you require this.

    Before making a decision, the District Valuer will consider any representations from you and the landlord and will reach a decision within 4 weeks of your written request for the revaluation.

3. Under s125(D) and (E) of the Housing Act, you have 12 weeks from receipt of this Notice, or of any revaluation notice under Item 2 above, to decide if you wish to exercise your Right to Buy. Your decision must be provided to the landlord in writing.

    If you fail to serve notice, the landlord may at any time after the end of the 12 week period, serve a further notice on you requiring you to respond within 28 days. If you do not respond within this period, upon its expiry your claim to exercise the Right to Buy will be deemed to have expired.

4. In accordance with s136(2) of the Housing Act 1985, if this Notice has been served on the previous tenant, then whether or not that tenant has served the RTB/RTA 3 Notice on the landlord, you as the new tenant must do so within the same period.

5. Where the landlord has agreed your Right to Buy they are required to complete the sale, and grant the lease as soon as all relevant matters have been settled. The landlord may serve a notice (under section 140 and 141 of the Housing Act 1985) requiring you to complete the transaction within a stated period (at least 56 days). The landlord cannot serve the notice to complete earlier than a year after the section 125 notice. The notice may not be served if a requirement for a valuation by the District Valuer has not been complied with, and not if there are any relevant matters outstanding.

    If you do not comply with the landlord's first notice to complete, they may serve a further notice giving you at least a further 56 days to complete the transaction.

6. Your liability to contribute to the estimated costs of day to day repairs and maintenance and to the charges for the itemised works described in this Notice is limited under Schedule 6 (16b) of the Housing Act 1985, to the amounts shown in this Notice for the "Reference Period" of the lease. The "Reference Period" will be 5 years commencing from the date of this s125 Notice. Therefore, you will not need to pay more than the costs quoted in this Notice for these items, plus an allowance for inflation.

7. Please do not hesitate to contact the Sales Officer, (Name) if you have any questions about the information contained in this notice.

❑ 4.8 Further reading on sales and section 125 notices

The Association of Retirement Housing Managers (ARHM) – for Code of Practice, revised edition due spring 2004, also good practice notes for members
www.arhm.org

Right to Buy leases – follow provisions specified in Schedule 6 Housing Act 1985

The Housing Corporation *Circular F2 68/89* announced the sample leases most commonly used by housing associations

The Housing Corporation (HC) – Regulatory Code and guidance, circulars, information, inspection reports
www.housingcorp.gov.uk

Office of the Deputy Prime Minister (ODPM) website for news and downloadable documents regarding leasehold issues
www.housing.odpm.gov.uk/information/leaseholdreform

Housing Act 1985 s125

Housing (PRTB) Regulations 1993 (SI 1993 No 2241)
Housing (PRTB) Amendment Regulations 1999 (SI 1999 No 1213) – also useful search engine on the website for Statutory Instruments
www.legislation.hmso.gov.uk

ODPM housing booklets – on the Right to Buy and other help to buy
www.odpm.gov.uk

The Housing Corporation (2003) *A Charter for Housing Association Applicants and Residents* August 2003
The Housing Corporation *Leaseholders Guarantee* – out of date but may be specified in some leases

Council of Mortgage Lenders *How to buy a home in England and Wales* – 'everything you need to know about mortgages, conveyancing, insurance and budget planning' – consumer advice produced by the CML
www.cml.org.uk

Citizens Advice (formerly CAB) – buying a home, mortgage advice
www.adviceguide.org.uk

Haley, Michael *Which? way to buy and sell a flat*
Which? consumer guides ISBN 08502 803 2

Living in Leasehold – LEASE and ARMA leaflet
www.lease-advice.org.uk

HOMES – shared ownership – details of new and resales properties – existing shared owners can use for resales with landlord's permission
www.homes.org.uk
The facilitated mobility service for shared ownership currently provided by HOMES is subject to change from 2004. Details on ODPM website.

CHAPTER 5

SERVICE CHARGING

This chapter deals with the day-to-day service charges that mainly recur each year.

It sets out the legal and regulatory requirements and the management arrangements necessary for the effective charging of service costs.

It sets out Housing Corporation, Government and other statutory guidance.

It explains the annual cycle of estimating, demanding, accounting and certification of service charges.

It deals with reserve funds, service charge loans, powers to reduce or waive service charges, consulting recognised residents' associations, insurance and management and administration charges, and the circumstances in which a leaseholder can withhold payment of service charges.

It provides guidance on assessing the service charge requirements of schemes at the design stage.

Service charging in respect of major works and improvements, and the associated consultation requirements are dealt with Chapter 6.

5.1 Legal requirements

■ Introduction

The rights of leaseholders and the duties of their landlords in relation to service charges are drawn together in the Landlord and Tenant Act 1985 and extended by the Landlord and Tenant Act 1987, the Leasehold Reform, Housing and Urban Development Act 1993, the Housing Act 1996 and the Commonhold and Leasehold Reform Act 2002.

The Landlord and Tenant Act 1985 introduced a single code for service charges payable under leases, whether for flats or for houses, and applies to both the public and private sectors.

The majority of local authorities leases have been created under the Right to Buy provisions of the Housing Acts, and the Housing Act 1985 is often referred to as the point of definition for service charge requirements. However, the requirements included in that Act are simply a restatement of those contained in the Landlord and Tenant Acts, now significantly amended by the Commonhold and Leasehold Reform Act 2002.

Housing association and local authority landlords considering the introduction of variable service charges for periodic tenants as a result of rent restructuring should bear in mind that the legislation will also apply to those tenancies.

The main points of legislation in relation to service charges are set out below:

■ The definition of a service charge

The definition of a service charge

1. Under s18 of the Landlord and Tenant Act 1985, a service charge is defined as an amount payable by a relevant tenant of a dwelling as part of, or in addition to, rent

2. Which is payable, directly or indirectly, for services, repairs, maintenance, *improvements* or insurance or the landlord's costs of management; and

3. The whole or part of which varies or may vary according to the relevant costs

NB: The Commonhold and Leasehold Reform Act 2002 added *"Improvements"* to s18

Service charges are not limited to day to day services but include the recovery of costs for major works to the fabric of the building and communal areas of a block or estate.

The 'relevant costs' can be either the actual costs, or estimated costs (including overheads) currently being incurred or that have already been incurred, or which may in the future be incurred, by the landlord or a superior landlord in connection with matters described in the definitions above.

The purpose of the definition in the legislation is to enable leaseholders to challenge service charges. It should be noted that legislation only enables service charge provisions to be made in leases, but that they cannot actually be recovered unless the terms of the lease provide for this.

It should also be noted that service charges relate to actual or estimated costs only, and there can be no element of profit built in to the recovery of the costs of services. In the private sector the landlord's profit will be obtained from the management fee component of the charge.

■ Service charges and the 18 month limit on costs

Section 20B of the Landlord and Tenant Act 1985 requires that any relevant costs included in a service charge must have been incurred within the 18 months before the service charge demand is made, otherwise the leaseholder cannot be required to pay.

The only exception to this is if, within 18 months of the costs being incurred, the landlord advises the leaseholder that the costs have been incurred, and that the leaseholder will be required to contribute towards them in the future.

It is important to note that the 18 month period begins from the date the relevant costs are incurred, and this has been established in case law to be the date when the obligation to make each payment comes into existence. This is particularly important where the relevant costs are incurred under a contract that provides for interim payments at certain stages of the works. In this case, the 18 month period will run from the date the first interim payment becomes due under the contract.

Therefore, if there is any likelihood of the final service charge demand being served more than 18 months after the first payment, then an interim notice should be served under s20B (2) containing the information set out above.

....

The 18 month rule and the Westminster ruling

Westminster City Council v BJ Hammond and others [1995] related to works which were carried out under a lump sum contract. The contract provided for interim payments at certain stages of the works with a final adjustment payment to be made once the Architect's final certificate had been issued.

The court held that for the purposes of s20B (1) the relevant costs are incurred when the obligation to make each payment comes into existence.

The court also held that in order to constitute proper notice under s20B (2) the notice had to give similar information to an actual demand - ie:
- The fact that relevant costs had been incurred (in this case the amount of the interim payments which had become payable up to that date);
- The nature of the works and reason for the expenditure;
- The amount of the costs incurred and the proportion attributable to the individual leasehold and;
- That such amount would be demanded at some stage in the future.

....

■ Landlord's name and address

Under s47 and s48 of the Landlord and Tenant Act 1987, a demand for rent or service charges must contain the name and address of the landlord. Failure to include this information makes the amount payable irrecoverable by the landlord until the landlord does comply.

■ The reasonableness of service charges

Under s19 of the Landlord and Tenant Act 1985 service charge costs must be reasonably incurred and the services or works must be to a reasonable standard. A leaseholder or a landlord can apply to have the following matters determined by a court or a Leasehold Valuation Tribunal (LVT):

- Whether costs incurred for services, repairs, maintenance, insurance or management were reasonably incurred;
- Whether services or works for which costs were incurred are of a reasonable standard; or
- Whether an amount payable before costs are incurred is reasonable.

The Commonhold and Leasehold Reform Act 2002 extended the jurisdiction of LVTs to also include:

- Whether a charge is payable or not
- By whom it is payable
- To whom it is payable
- The amount that is payable
- The date by which it is payable
- The manner in which it is payable

Chapter 11 of this guide covers the operation of LVTs.

■ Providing a summary of relevant service charge costs

Under s21 of the Landlord and Tenant Act 1985 leaseholders could request a written summary of costs incurred by the landlord and for which a charge is payable or has been demanded.

Many managers provided regular statements of account as a matter of good practice (as recommended in the RICS and ARHM codes) but this was never a legal requirement unless the terms of the lease demanded accounts.

Section 152 of the Commonhold and Leasehold Reform Act 2002 has amended s21 of the 1985 Act to formalise the right to be provided with this information without having to request it.

The landlord must supply to each leaseholder a regular statement of account for each accounting period, setting out:

- The service charges the individual leaseholder must pay
- The total service charges for the group of properties involved
- The relevant costs relating to those service charges
- The aggregate amount standing to the credit of the tenant and the tenants of those dwellings:
  (i) at the beginning of the accounting period, and
  (ii) at the end of the accounting period, and

the statement of account in relation to an accounting period must be supplied to the leaseholder not later than six months after the end of the accounting period.

The landlord must also supply:

- A certificate of a qualified accountant that, in the accountant's opinion, the statement of account deals fairly with the matters with which it is required to deal and is sufficiently supported by accounts, receipts and other documents which have been produced to the accountant
- A summary of the rights and obligations of the leaseholders of dwellings in relation to service charges

If the leaseholder has notified the landlord, or the landlord's agent, of another address (in England and Wales) to which this information should be supplied, the landlord must supply them at that address. This is important where the leaseholder has sub-let the property, or where the landlord has contracted out the housing management functions.

Under s152 of the Commonhold and Leasehold Reform Act 2002, the leaseholder is able to withhold payment of the service charges if the landlord has not supplied accounting statements in accordance with s21 of the 1985 Act.

The Secretary of State may make regulations prescribing requirements as to the form and content of:

- Statements of account,
- Accountants' certificates
- Summaries of rights and obligations.

The Secretary of State may also make regulations prescribing exceptions from the requirement to supply an accountant's certificate.

At the time of writing the final regulations have not been published, but it is clear that the prescribed format for service charge accounts will mean change for many managers as it will involve showing income received as well as receivable and a balance sheet of some kind showing reserve funds held, as well as separation of s20 works costs in the income and expenditure account.

■ Certification of accounts

If the service charges are payable by the residents of more than four dwellings, s28 of the Landlord and Tenant Act 1985 currently requires that the summary of accounts requested under s21 must be certified by a 'qualified accountant'. This is replaced in the 2002 Act by the requirement that a regular statement of account in a prescribed form, still to be published, must be provided, together with an accountant's certificate, which is subject to any exceptions prescribed by the Secretary of State.

The meaning of qualified accountant is contained in s28 of the 1985 Act and requires that for all landlords other than local authorities, the 'qualified accountant' must be independent of the landlord. Local authorities may rely upon a suitably qualified accountant employed by them.

It is common practice for a registered social landlord to use their external auditors for this purpose.

A sample of certified accounts that comply with the Act can be found in the NHF publication *Service Charges – a guide for Registered Social Landlords* (March 2003).

Whilst some groups of property may comprise fewer than four dwellings, landlords often generally require their auditors to certify all the service charge accounts rather than only those for larger blocks.

■ Request to inspect supporting information to the statement of account

Under s22 of the Landlord and Tenant Act 1985, within six months of receiving the summary of relevant costs, a leaseholder or secretary of a recognised residents association can ask to be given reasonable facilities to inspect, or make copies of, all the accounts, receipts and other documentation that support the summary.

This request must be in writing, and the landlord must make the facilities available within 21 days, under an amendment contained in the Commonhold and Leasehold Reform Act 2002. The amendment also introduced the right for leaseholders to request that copies of supporting information be sent to them.

There must be no direct charge for inspecting the documentation, but the costs incurred in making the facilities available can be treated as a management cost and included in the service charge. Leaseholders should be allowed to take, or be sent, copies of any item and a reasonable charge can be made for that.

■ The right to an independent management audit

Section 76 of the Leasehold Reform, Housing and Urban Development Act 1993 gives leaseholders the right to carry out a management audit. The purpose of the audit is to examine whether or not the landlord is managing in an efficient and effective way and whether service charges are being properly administered.

This right applies where:

- There are more than two leaseholders in a premises
- More than two thirds of the leaseholders want an audit, or one leaseholder where there are only two involved.

The auditor can require the landlord to:

- Supply a summary of service charge costs for the most recent period under s21 of the Landlord & Tenant Act 1985
- Allow inspection of supporting accounts, receipts and documentation and allow facilities for copying.

In order to exercise the right to the management audit:

- Leaseholders must appoint, at their own expense, an auditor who is a qualified accountant, valuer or surveyor and who is not one of the leaseholders concerned; and
- Serve a notice under section 80 of the 1993 Act signed by all the leaseholders who want the audit. The notice must give the names and addresses of the leaseholders and the auditor, and specify the documents the auditor wishes to see. If an inspection is carried out, a date should be proposed by the leaseholders or their auditor of between one and two months from the date of service of the notice.

■ Requests for information held by a superior landlord

Where a landlord is not the freeholder, but is head leaseholder or next immediate landlord, the freeholder or head leaseholder is known as the superior landlord. In such cases leaseholders or the secretary of a recognised residents' association can request a summary of relevant costs and inspections of documents from their immediate landlord or that landlord's managing agent in accordance with s23 of the Landlord and Tenant Act 1985.

Any requests for a summary must be passed on by the immediate landlord to the superior landlord who must comply within a reasonable time. The information received from the superior landlord must then be passed on to the leaseholder.

The immediate landlord should supply the leaseholder with the name and address of the superior landlord if they wish to inspect documentation.

■ Failure to comply with requests for cost summary or inspection

If a landlord fails to comply with requests for a summary of costs or does not provide facilities for inspecting accounts, it is a criminal offence under s25 of the Landlord and Tenant Act 1985 for which a fine can be levied up to level 4 on the standard scale (currently £2,500).

Whilst local authorities are exempt from this criminal offence, housing associations are not. It is vital to have procedures to record requests from leaseholders for cost information for monitoring responses.

■ Residents' associations' rights to appoint a surveyor to advise on service charge matters

The Housing Act 1996 gave residents' associations the right to appoint a qualified surveyor to advise on any matters relating to service charges. The powers of the qualified surveyor are set out in Schedule 4 of the 1996 Act. Landlords are required to allow access to relevant documents to any such qualified surveyor appointed by a residents' association.

A qualified surveyor in this instance could be an accountant, valuer or surveyor qualified to carry out a management audit, as outlined above.

■ Insurance

The Landlord and Tenant Act 1987 introduced a schedule into the Landlord and Tenant Act 1985 which gives leaseholders rights in respect of insurance. These have been enhanced by the CLRA 2002. The principal rights are set out below:

- **Written summary of insurance cover**
  The Commonhold and Leasehold Reform Act 2002 (Schedule 10) requires that, if requested by a leaseholder or a recognised residents' association, landlords must provide a written summary of insurance cover within 21 days stating the amount insured, the name of the insurer and the insured risks. Instead of the summary the landlord may alternatively supply a copy of the policy.

- **Inspection of policy**
  Provisions in the Commonhold and Leasehold Reform Act 2002 enable a leaseholder or residents' association to request to inspect the policy without having first requested a summary of it. Both may request an opportunity to inspect the policy and any associated documents including evidence of payment of the premium and take copies of the documents or require that copies are made available for collection or sent to them.

  The landlord must make the facilities available within 21 days (Schedule 10 para.9) and allow them to be available for two months. A reasonable charge can be made for the taking of any copies.

- **Notifying insurers of potential claims**
  Leaseholders have the right to notify the insurer directly of any damage to the dwelling or the building although not the right to make a claim.
- **Challenge landlord's choice of insurer**
  If a leaseholder is required to insure their dwelling with an insurer nominated by the landlord and he/she considers the premium excessive or the insurance is unsatisfactory, he/she can request the county court, or under the Housing Act 1996, a Leasehold Valuation Tribunal to make an order to the landlord to nominate another insurer.

■ Insurance otherwise than with landlord's insurer for leaseholders of houses

Leases sometimes require the leaseholder to insure the property with an insurer nominated or approved by the landlord.

Under s164 of the Commonhold and Leasehold Reform Act, leaseholders of *houses* will no longer have to do this, as long as they arrange their insurance with an insurer authorised under section 19 of the Financial Services and Markets Act 2000, and satisfy certain requirements, such as notifying the landlord within a certain period of time. A Commencement Order implementing this is expected in mid 2004.

The policy must cover the interests of both the landlord and the leaseholder for all the risks and level of cover required under the lease.

Section 164 also sets out detailed requirements in respect of the form of notice that must be given to the landlord.

■ Recognised residents' associations' rights to be consulted about managing agents

Under s30B of the Landlord and Tenant Act 1985, a recognised residents' association can serve a notice on the landlord requesting him/her to consult the residents' association on the appointment or employment of a managing agent. This is dealt with in more detail in Chapter 10 of this guide.

The legislation sets out the requirements of the notices and the timescales for the process.

■ Right to a service charge loan

Under the Housing (Service Charge Loans) Regulations 1992 SI 1992 No 1708 as amended by SI 2000 No 163 leaseholders who have bought under the Right to Buy provisions of the Housing Act 1985 have the right to a loan from the landlord in the case of local authorities, and from the Housing Corporation (see HC Circular 01/03) in the case of housing associations, within the first ten years of their lease (these regulations *do not* apply to purchasers under the PRTB or RTA). The conditions are as follows:

- The total service charge demand in any one year is more than £1,900. In this context 'service charge demand' includes contributions to major works;
- The minimum amount of loan is currently £640 and the maximum £25,250, adjusted annually by reference to the RPI;
- Leaseholders must be informed of their right to a loan when sent a service charge demand; and
- Loans are only available for charges relating to repairs, currently, but this is extended to include improvements as a result of the extension of the meaning of 'service charge' in the Commonhold and Leasehold Reform Act 2002 Schedule 9 s2(2).

The loans must be repaid within three to ten years (depending on the amount of the loan) and interest is charged at the local authority mortgage interest rate in the case of local authority lessees.

■ Power to reduce or waive service charges

The Housing Act 1996 gave the Secretary of State the power to issue directions that will allow, and in some cases require, social landlords to waive or reduce service charges in certain circumstances.

The Social Landlords Mandatory Reduction of Service Charges (England) Directions 1997 *require* the reduction of service charges for repairs, maintenance or improvements carried out wholly or partly with assistance from the Single Regeneration (SRB) Challenge Fund or from the Estates Renewal Challenge Fund (ERCF) where,

- Assistance is applied for on or after February 25, 1997, *and*
- If charges for the same leasehold property exceed £10,000 in any five-year period.

This has subsequently been extended to cover funding under the New Deal for Communities (15 August 1999) and the Private Finance Initiative (17 January 2000).

Under the Social Landlords Discretionary Reduction of Service Charges (England) Directions 1997 social landlords *may* reduce or waive service charges for past, current and future works of repair, maintenance or improvement:

- If carried out wholly or partly with assistance under Estate Action, City Challenge, the SRB Challenge Fund, or ERCF, where assistance was applied for before February 25, 1997; *or,*
- Where the total service charges are more than £10,000 in any five-year period for the same leasehold property, *no matter how the works were funded*.

The costs of reducing or waiving charges are borne by the landlord – no Government assistance is given.

Again this has subsequently been extended to cover funding under the New Deal for Communities and the Private Finance Initiative.

More guidance on the operation of mandatory and discretionary service charge reductions is provided in Chapter 6 of this guide.

■ Recognising residents' associations

The Landlord and Tenant Acts allow for the formal recognition of residents' associations and give recognised residents' associations specific rights to be consulted on service charge matters.

❏ 5.2 Contractual considerations in relation to service charges

The liability of leaseholders to financially contribute to any of the landlord's costs is ultimately dependent upon there being provision in the lease allowing the landlord to charge for those services or supplies to which the costs relate. This is one of the least understood aspects of leasehold ownership and one which accordingly results in many disputes and difficulties.

Individual leases will include explicit requirements in relation to services, service charges and service charge payments. These must be referred to regularly to ensure they are being adhered to. Among the provisions that may be included are:

- The provision of services, the costs of which can be recovered
- How service charges are to be calculated and apportioned
- The periods for which accounts are to be prepared
- The arrangements for collection and payment of the service charge
- The auditing and certification of annual accounts
- The treatment of surpluses or deficits

There are three fundamental points to remember:

Key points on recovering service charges

- the landlord can only recover costs for services if there is provision within the lease;
- if the landlord provides services additional to those in the lease, the costs may not be recoverable;
- the landlord is obliged to provide the services specified in the lease.

Many service charge disputes concern the inadequacy of services provided by the landlord in the view of the leaseholder, and in such circumstances it may be reasonable for the landlord to consider reducing or even waiving a charge where a clear failure of service becomes apparent.

In order to resist claims that a service has been inadequate it will be necessary for the landlord to produce evidence that the quality, frequency or level of service justifies the charge being made. This means having monitoring systems in place, including regular inspections before payments are made to contractors.

Leaseholders may only register their dissatisfaction with the service when they receive their demands or accounts, which may be months after the landlord or managing agent has paid the contractor concerned. By then it will be too late to reclaim payments from the contractor or to recover the costs from leaseholders.

Leaseholders cannot completely avoid payment simply because a service was inadequate – in *Yorkbrook Investment v Batten [1985]*, the court held that the wording of the Landlord and Tenant Act 1985 does not require an 'all or nothing' approach, and that the landlord can apply a proportionate reduction in the charge.

■ Variation of services

A major issue for management of leasehold properties is how to deal with amendments to services. The amendment may involve an increased or decreased level of service or the provision of a new service, and may be at the landlord's behest, or that of a group of leaseholders.

How easily and effectively such amendments to contracts can be made depends in part on what is to be changed, but also on the provisions of the individual lease. Some leases provide for amendments to services under certain circumstances such as following consultation and with the agreement of leaseholders.

The new version of the ARHM code has a recommended procedure for varying essential services on retirement schemes if the lease allows a change without a formal deed of variation. It is based on a voting procedure rather than normal consultation methods.

However, many leases do not contain such a provision and lock all parties into defined services for the length of lease. The only course of action that can be taken in these situations is to undertake a variation to the lease. Variations to leases are dealt with in Chapter 3.

❑ 5.3 Housing Corporation requirements

The Housing Corporation expects registered housing associations to comply with its Regulatory Code and the Charter for Housing Association Applicants and Residents.

■ Regulatory Code and Guidance

Some key points affecting service charges to note from the Regulatory Code

A self-assessment of compliance with the code has to be made and an annual compliance statement provided to the Housing Corporation.

Alongside this, inspections undertaken by the Audit Commission for the Housing Corporation will involve a substantial component of input from residents.

Inspectors will look at:

- The quality of information provided to leaseholders, particularly in respect of service costs and charges and how they are calculated
- How services are reviewed, challenged, and measured against national standards
- How services are shaped around customers' needs
- How performance is reported on to the governing body
- How the condition of stock is monitored and if satisfactory progress towards the Decent Homes Standard is maintained
- Whether sinking fund payments are held in trust

From April 2003 there is a distinction to be made between regulation, which remains the responsibility of the Housing Corporation and inspection, which is now undertaken by the Housing Inspectorate within the Audit Commission.

The self-assessment by housing associations of compliance is a regulatory matter. The Corporation's regulatory engagement is clarified and defined in Regulatory Code Good Practice Note Number 6 *Our Regulatory Engagement with Housing Associations* available on the Corporation's website.

In working with RSLs, the Inspectorate will not examine leasehold management in detail each time it inspects an association that happens to own some leasehold property. The current inspection framework focuses on six core service areas in each inspection, with some additional aspects looked at if resources permit, or if those additional areas represent a significant element of the landlord's business.

So, for example, an association owning a large number of retirement leasehold homes should expect to have its management of that stock included in inspections, whilst an association with a handful of RTB flats would probably not find this aspect under close review. However, in making an assessment of any aspect of an association's performance, eg in repairs or participation, the inspectors will take account of available evidence about the quality of service offered both to tenants and leaseholders.

■ A Charter for Housing Association Applicants and Residents

This replaces the former Leaseholders Guarantee and Shared Owners Charter and is designed to apply to all the customers of registered housing associations.

It should be noted that some existing leases refer to the Leaseholders Guarantee and form a contractual commitment by the association to continue to comply with the terms of the former Guarantee. It may also have been cited in stock transfer agreements which may similarly create a contractual obligation.

The new Charter does make specific reference to leaseholders in each section and associations must provide copies to all leaseholders.

❑ 5.4 Central Government requirements

Government guidance is limited to booklets for the benefit of leaseholders – all the existing ones are being revised and may be consolidated into a single volume. The Government has considered whether to publish a more detailed guide to the changes brought about by the Commonhold and Leasehold Reform Act 2002, but is likely to leave it to LEASE, which proposes publishing guidance at the end of 2003.

There is no proposal to provide further guidance to social landlords in respect of regeneration schemes, although the financial assistance guidance may be updated.

The Association of London Government is publishing guidance on council leasehold management at the end of 2003.

❑ 5.5 Other sources of service charge guidance

Both the Association of Retirement Housing Managers (ARHM) and Royal Institution of Chartered Surveyors (RICS) Codes of Guidance issued under the Leasehold Reform, Housing and Urban Development Act 1993 contain specimen and model accounts and budgets, as well as other guidance on the management of service charges.

❏ 5.6 Best value

There are currently no statutory best value performance indicators (PIs) and the Audit Commission has observed that many local authorities have not developed leasehold specific PIs nor included leasehold performance within other PIs.

Some performance indicators relating to service charges that the Audit Commission has indicated that it is likely to find acceptable when undertaking inspections of local authority and housing association landlords include:

- Percentage of service charge accounts issued within six months of the financial year end
- Average service charge
- Average increase / decrease in service charge
- Level of service charge arrears
  - As percentage of annual debit
  - Percentage of leaseholders owing over 13 weeks service charge
- Number of cases where section 146 notice served
- Amount and percentage of debt written off
- Percentage of leaseholders by type who are satisfied with their service charges, account and estimate information
- Number of referrals to Leasehold Valuation Tribunal for determination of reasonableness
- Percentage / number of leasehold properties on which planned / major works carried out during year

These are not the only PIs that should be used, and for example some additional PIs used by **Birmingham City Council** include:

- Number of leaseholders receiving each Head of Charge (Cleaning, Caretaking etc)
- Total raised per Head of Charge
- Average per Head of Charge
- Write offs/reductions in relation to each Head of Charge
- Number of leaseholders at 31 March each year

At the time of writing the Housing Corporation is developing a set of performance indicators for leasehold housing.

It is important that in planning best value strategies and programmes leasehold services are examined holistically. For example, service charges may be included in a best value review of income collection; s20 consultation may be examined in a maintenance review; and information to leaseholders in a communications review.

Such an approach is not wrong, but can lead to a failure to evaluate services to leaseholders as a whole. If leasehold management does not figure as a best value review area, then landlords undertaking best value review programmes need to ensure that all aspects of leasehold management are covered and that the outputs from several best value reviews are capable of being drawn together to provide a clear picture of the overall quality of the leasehold service.

❏ 5.7 The operation of service charges

This section examines the practical operation of a service charge regime based on the principles laid down in published guidance.

■ Annual service charge cycle

A good starting point is the timetable to be followed. This will vary amongst landlords only in so far as the payment demand dates of individual leases differ.

The main stages of the annual service charge timetable (for an April to March accounting year)	
Estimate service charges for the next year	Nov - Dec
Send estimates and annual service charge demand to leaseholders	February for payment by (per lease)
Close accounts and preparation of service charge actuals	April - June
Audit certification of service charge statements	July - Aug
Send out service charge statements with covering letter and details of any adjustments	Aug - Sept

■ Annual service charge process

See the diagram on the next page.

❏ 5.8 Estimating service costs (service charge budgeting)

It is important to remember that within the landlord's property portfolio individual schemes may have their own leases with different definitions of services that can be charged for, different methods of apportioning costs and other provisions that require variation from any standard approach to service charging that the landlord may adopt. Specific components of a service charge (heads of charge) can only be recovered in respect of a property if the lease for that property provides for the recovery of the cost of that service component.

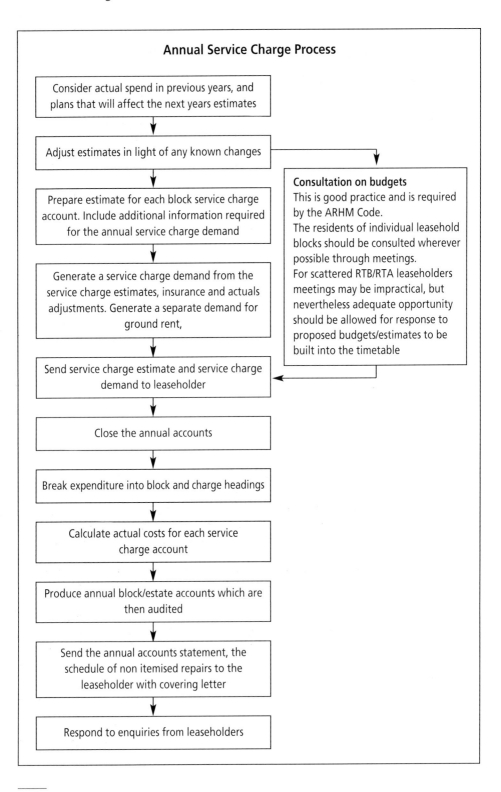

Annual Service Charge Process

Consider actual spend in previous years, and plans that will affect the next years estimates

↓

Adjust estimates in light of any known changes

↓

Prepare estimate for each block service charge account. Include additional information required for the annual service charge demand

↓

Generate a service charge demand from the service charge estimates, insurance and actuals adjustments. Generate a separate demand for ground rent,

↓

Send service charge estimate and service charge demand to leaseholder

↓

Close the annual accounts

↓

Break expenditure into block and charge headings

↓

Calculate actual costs for each service charge account

↓

Produce annual block/estate accounts which are then audited

↓

Send the annual accounts statement, the schedule of non itemised repairs to the leaseholder with covering letter

↓

Respond to enquiries from leaseholders

Consultation on budgets
This is good practice and is required by the ARHM Code.
The residents of individual leasehold blocks should be consulted wherever possible through meetings.
For scattered RTB/RTA leaseholders meetings may be impractical, but nevertheless adequate opportunity should be allowed for response to proposed budgets/estimates to be built into the timetable

Basic procedures to follow for estimating costs

1. One basis for estimating service charges is to take the average actual expenditure for the previous two years uprated for inflation, increases in utility prices, and any other known changes such as may arise from contract renewals. This is still the most common approach amongst local authorities, however increasingly landlords are examining each budget line for each charge group of properties on an annual basis, and not simply making an increase in line with inflation. Applying best value principles to service charge estimating requires this approach anyway.

2. Where the lease arises as a result of a new RTB sale, then if another similar property in the same charge group has been sold within the previous two years the estimate should be based upon that other property. Where this is not possible, the estimate can be arrived at by using another leasehold property elsewhere of a similar size, type, age and location.

   For Right to Buy or Acquire sales, where there has not been a sale in the block before, information will be available from the s125 notice.

3. Estimates should take into account any changes to costs that are already known about. For example, if the grass cutting has been retendered, or if a door entry system has been installed and there is a new item to be added to the service charge for its maintenance.

4. Planned maintenance works due to be carried out in the coming year will also need to be identified and included in the estimate. A detailed breakdown of the works and their estimated cost for the next financial year should be provided in time for this to be incorporated in the service charge estimates. This may be in advance of the s20 consultation, which will still need to be undertaken at the appropriate time (see Chapter 7).

5. An estimate for each leasehold property, block and estate should be provided. The estimate must provide details of the expected charge under each of the service charge headings prescribed in the lease.

6. In the case of a Right to Buy or Acquire lease, where the lease is still within the initial 5 year period, the estimate for non itemised repairs and planned maintenance works must be checked against the amount quoted in the s125 notice uprated for inflation as allowed in the legislation. Where the estimated costs would exceed the limitation imposed by the s125 this must be noted and arrangements made to invoice only for the amount allowed by the notice although the estimate should still show the expected costs.

7. Other details required for the service charge demand should be collated at the same time as the estimate including any debit or credit from the previous years actuals and the insurance costs. Under new provisions in the Commonhold and Leasehold Reform Act 2002 it is likely that ground rent will have to be demanded separately from other charges.

The information required may be held in a bespoke system or a spreadsheet system. It is important that whatever system is used is properly maintained and contains all the details required.

■ Sending out the estimates

The service charge estimates and information relating to insurance and the actuals adjustments are used to generate an estimate and a service charge demand for each leaseholder. The estimates, service charge demand, standing order or direct debit form should then be sent to the individual leaseholder. The service charge demand must include:

- The landlord's name and address
- A brief explanation of the legal entitlement to a service charge loan for RTB leaseholders during the first 10 years of their lease
- An explanation of the payment expected
- Details of any schemes that the landlord may choose to offer to assist leaseholders to pay the service charge

Under provisions of the Commonhold and Leasehold Reform Act 2002, a statement of leaseholders' rights in the form prescribed under the Act will be required once the format has been published in a Commencement Order in mid 2004.

If the estimate varies from the amount demanded because of the limitations imposed by a s125 notice this should also be explained. The demand must give clear details of who the leaseholder should contact if they have any queries about the account or how to pay.

Bromford Housing Group – lease summaries

The association places a lease summary at the front of each scheme service charge file to provide an 'at a glance' guide to assist staff to ensure service charges are administered correctly.

The general format is as follows:

Clause	Summary	Section in lease
Property type		
Term of lease		
Ground rent		
Assignment clause		
Admin. fee for assignment		
Contribution to service charge		
Lessee repairing obligations		
Lessor repairing obligations		
Cyclical painting frequency		
Reserves contribution		

This approach is best suited to schemes that have been specifically built to house leaseholders, rather than schemes with scattered RTB leaseholders that may not all have identical provisions in their leases.

❑ 5.9 Compiling the statement of account

Once the accounts are closed, the actual service charge costs to be charged to each leaseholder can be calculated.

Tracking expenditure

Cost coding systems must enable costs to be accumulated by individual blocks of homes and estates, as well as under expenditure headings that reflect the requirements of the leases held by residents of those blocks.

For some types of expenditure there may only be one expenditure code, for others, a number of different codes may be used for types of work and these will need to be grouped together to produce the overall total under the main charge heading.

Expenditure under each heading will need to be split between estate and building costs apportioned in accordance with the requirements of the lease. If it is not specific within the lease then a fair and reasonable approach should be used.

There should be consistency from year to year in the method of apportioning estate costs unless it is clear that the method in use will not produce a fair and reasonable result.

Where jobs are not to be charged to the leaseholder, for example if it is known that the work was unsatisfactory or the cost should have been claimed on insurance, a record should be kept with an explanation of the reasons for the decision not to charge. Similarly where work has been miscoded and is corrected by moving it to a different block or charge heading, a record of that action should be kept. It must always be possible to reconcile the payments to be charged and those to be omitted or reallocated with the original cost of works relating to that block.

It is important to check that repairs ordered on the maintenance system have been coded to the correct location, and that the works are rechargeable to the leaseholder. Maintenance staff may need to assist with the correct apportionment of costs, where this isn't obvious to the leasehold manager. Checks should also be made that repairs undertaken as part of day-to-day maintenance have not breached s20 consultation limits.

Expenditure under other heads of charge will mostly be derived from service contracts. For each head of charge the contract sum will need to be broken down and apportioned. A check should be made that payments have been made as required by the contract and that there have been no duplicate payments. Where an adjustment to the charges has been agreed because of a failure to provide a service, check that this has been carried out.

→

There are always likely to be some 'one off' items of expenditure, which are not within service contracts. For example major tree work may not covered by the grounds maintenance contract. Each of these items of expenditure will be added to the block listing under the head of charge to which they relate, and the individual works orders should be traced and checked in the same manner as for day-to-day repairs. A record should be kept of the checks made and any decisions not to recharge the costs. Any inability to recharge should be monitored and taken into account when considering any updating or revision of the master lease.

■ Presenting the information

The information should be tabulated to give a listing for each block and estate giving the total actual expenditure for the previous year split into sub-totals for each of the individual heads of charge. This information is then used to calculate the expenditure for each individual leaseholder by applying the apportionment method prescribed in the lease, or using other appropriate methods of apportionment to arrive at a fair and reasonable split of the block, estate and other costs.

Under new provisions of the Commonhold and Leasehold Reform Act 2002, leaseholders must be given a written statement of account showing the service charges for the individual leaseholder and all the leaseholders of any associated dwellings, as well as relevant costs relating to the service charges and the aggregate amount standing to the credit of the individual leaseholder and to all leaseholders of the dwellings, both at the beginning and the end of the accounting period.

❑ 5.10 The end of year reconciliation

The actual expenditure for each leaseholder should be compared with the estimate for that year to arrive at the figure by which the leaseholder has been over or under charged.

An actuals statement (this is the end of year accounts) for each leaseholder should be sent with a covering letter explaining whether any adjustment needed because of over or under estimation of the service charge will be included in the next invoice, or demanded or refunded at once. The lease may prescribe how under and over payments are to be dealt with, and this must be complied with. If the lease is not specific then the reasonableness criteria of s19(2) of the Landlord and Tenant Act 1985 should be complied with. It is not good practice to add surpluses to reserve funds or to use them to create reserve funds (*St Mary's Mansions v Limegate Investments Ltd [Court of Appeal] 2002*) and leases may not in fact permit it.

Where the actual amount expended on non-itemised repairs or programmed works has not been recovered because of the limitations imposed by a s125 notice, this should also be explained in the actuals statement or covering letter.

If items in the demand are based on estimates rather than actual costs, this should be made clear.

A covering letter should contain clear details of who the leaseholder should contact if they have any queries, and under new provisions in the Commonhold and Leasehold Reform Act 2002, must also contain a statement of the leaseholder's rights in respect of service charges. The prescribed form for this will be contained in the Commencement Order expected in mid 2004.

It is inevitable that when service charge estimates, demands and accounts are sent out there is a surge of activity as queries are raised by leaseholders. It is important to ensure resources are available to deal with this peak period of activity, and that staff have ready access to financial information and copies of leases in order to respond efficiently. In larger leasehold blocks another option is to call a meeting at which a presentation on the accounts statement can be made. At such a meeting a file of the supporting invoices and receipts should be taken along and made available to leaseholders to inspect.

❏ 5.11 Service charges on mixed tenure housing schemes

On mixed tenure estates the same base of cost information will be used to create service charges for rent paying tenants, although only some of the costs chargeable to leaseholders are recoverable through service charges to rented tenancies, the others being part of the dwelling rental.

The key point to remember is that the full costs of those services that are charged to both leaseholders and other tenants are fully recovered, and on an equitable basis. It should be remembered that failure to collect the full costs chargeable to leaseholders could result in other tenants bearing costs disproportionately.

Service costing systems need to be developed in a manner that serves both lease and tenancy agreement requirements. Where a service-costing system used for rented properties does not meet the legal obligations to the leaseholders, then the landlord will have to change the costing system.

❑ 5.12 Service charges to freeholders

Some sales under both Right to Purchase schemes and shared ownership will be of freehold houses on mixed tenure estates, but where there are service charge covenants in place to cover the costs of estate grounds maintenance and other matters. All the same principles in these cases will need to be applied as described above.

Landlords selling houses on estates should ensure that suitable service charge covenants are included at the point of sale, so that service charge costs are capable of recovery in appropriate circumstances. This is usually done by the reservation of a rent charge or the requirement of any purchaser to enter into a Deed of Covenant before becoming registered at HM Land Registry.

❑ 5.13 Reserve funds and sinking funds

■ The purpose of sinking funds, reserve funds and depreciation funds

Some leases allow for a fund to be created, to build up sums to pay for large, infrequent items of expenditure, such as replacing a lift or refurbishing a roof, or for major items which occur regularly, such as redecoration. These funds may be referred to in leases by a variety of terms, but the intention in their creation is generally the same.

The usefulness of these funds is in spreading costs between successive residents, to avoid the risks of work not being carried out for lack of funds, or of current residents being faced with large bills for infrequent works.

The value of such funds is that money is accumulated collectively, so that even if a resident lives at a property for only a short period, the value of their property is enhanced at sale by the extent of provision for the future.

The lease may specify how contributions to such funds should be calculated. Further guidance is given below.

In the operation of sinking funds and designated reserve funds it is important to ensure that peaks and troughs within the fund do not produce unmanageable deficits or surpluses, and yet provide adequate money when required. These funds are helpful to residents and landlords, but managing them is a specialised task, requiring careful planning and monitoring.

Many landlords hold funds of this type, but can only do so if permitted by the lease – see box below.

The Housing Corporation refers to sinking funds rather than reserve funds and regards it as a matter of good practice for housing associations to have a sinking fund where the lease permits its establishment. They regard it as key to an association's asset management strategy to make proper provision for the future, and this includes setting up sinking funds wherever possible.

The Corporation also requires that sinking fund payments should be held in trust. The ARHM has produced guidance on the tax implications of this.

The landlord's ability to create a reserve fund

The most important point to remember is that the ability to create a reserve fund and the expenditure for which it may be used is governed by the provisions of the lease, and that a legal interpretation of what is possible under the terms of existing leases will usually be needed.

The questions to be asked are:

- Can reserve fund contributions be collected?

- For what items is it permissible to collect reserve fund contributions?

- Upon what basis should future expenditure on these items be estimated?

Note also that if the lease requires the collection of reserve fund contributions by using words such as 'shall' or 'will', then the landlord must do so for the protection of future lessees.

Leases may not refer explicitly to reserve or sinking funds, but may include a provision that includes both current and future works in the costs that may be charged to the leaseholder. This enables the landlord to create a Reserve Fund.

If the lease only refers to expenditure to be incurred in the next 12 months and does not refer to future works and costs, then it is unlikely that the landlord will be able to set up a reserve fund, unless all leaseholders agree. In all cases checking the lease is essential before attempting to create a reserve fund for the first time.

The principal requirements that must be met by reserve funds

The aim is to ensure that peaks and troughs within the fund do not produce abnormal or unmanageable deficits or surpluses and yet provide adequate money for works when required. They are helpful to both leaseholders and landlords, but need careful planning and properly resourced monitoring.

- The contributions should be reasonable. This means that they should be based upon real information about property condition and the life cycle of building components.

- The amount charged annually should be based upon the expected cost of each item of major repair and renewal divided by the number of years that will elapse before the work is carried out. These separate costs should be added together to produce the annual charge. The Government recommends that, to ensure contributions are in line with expected future levels of expenditure, local authorities should from time to time review programmes and their costs. Reserve fund provisions should be reviewed regularly, perhaps every two or three years to reappraise the fund in the light of ageing of the building.

- Calculations on reserve funds should be scheme specific and not cover several estates or blocks unless the works proposed are exactly the same.

- As the amounts collected are in advance of the work being undertaken, it is necessary to adjust future charges if the actual cost of the work is less or more than the estimate upon which the charge was based.

- It is recommended practice for local authorities to include a statement relating to the proposed provision for reserve funds or designated reserve funds in the s125 notice.

Estimating the scale of future expenditure is always difficult and leaseholders can challenge the reasonableness of reserve fund contributions if they feel they are excessive. Estimates for the replacement costs of building components should therefore be based on recognised indices such as Spons Price Book, and justified by reference to stock condition survey information.

Section 42 of the Landlord and Tenant Act 1987 requires private landlords to set up trust funds to hold any amounts collected from leaseholders as service charge contributions including reserve fund contributions. Whilst housing associations and local authorities are not bound by this requirement, Housing Corporation Regulatory Guidance requires 'sinking' fund payments to be held in Trust by registered associations as well.

■ Reserve funds for newly developed leasehold schemes

Because reserve funds have the advantage of requiring a relatively small payment each month, which can avoid large bills in the future, some housing associations use this as a selling point to prospective leaseholders as it can clearly be regarded as an insurance against future large repair costs.

Some associations separate out reserve funds for cyclical decoration and associated repairs from major works and renewals eg roofs, windows, and lifts. Following consultation with leaseholders and if the lease permits it, some associations have opted to charge only for the cyclical fund and not for the repair/renewal elements as leaseholders have expressed a preference for obtaining further mortgages to fund the lump sums required.

Again, reserve funds can only be included or dispensed with as part of the service charge if a lease provides for it.

■ Reserve funds for older properties sold under the various right to purchase schemes

Reserve funds for older flats purchased either through Right To Buy, Right to Acquire or shared ownership are less easy to achieve.

Often major works are required before reserve funds have had time to build up and leaseholders are still required to make large single payments.

Some transfer associations have introduced new leases that do allow for reserve funds and therefore have to deal with leaseholders in different situations when major works are planned. In effect reserve funds become individual savings accounts and separate calculations of the contribution from each property should be kept. It is wrong to assume that each leaseholder in a block has an equal proportionate share of reserve funds collected on RTB properties.

This can lead to financial, administrative and management problems, and confused and dissatisfied leaseholders. The benefits of reserve fund contributions for RTB and RTA properties are therefore not clear cut and cannot be clearly recommended as good practice in all circumstances.

In addition, many Right to Buy leases do not provide for the collection of a reserve fund. In those circumstances, and where the landlord chooses not to collect reserve fund contributions, the leaseholders should be given an annually updated 5 year forecast for the cost of major works to their homes, and be urged to set money aside to meet the costs when they are billed.

See also Chapter 9.1 on assistance to leaseholders with the cost of major works.

■ The calculation of reserve fund contributions

Future costs should be based on life cycle costing. The easiest way to do this is to estimate the life of each building component and the replacement cost and to schedule these for each block involved. These schedules should be reviewed on a regular basis in the light of surveys, and the costs amended accordingly.

It may be necessary to increase the leaseholders' contributions if it becomes apparent that more work is required than was anticipated, or if it becomes clear that it is required earlier than planned.

A cash flow for each block should show money contributed, interest on unused sums and the years when money will be expended.

It is important to recognise that reserve funds require regular review and should not just be set at the handover of a scheme and then forgotten.

■ The management of reserve funds

The creation and control of reserve funds is a sophisticated technical and financial task. It is necessary to take into account the effects of inflation, the actual cash flow in and out of funds and the accumulation of interest when calculating amounts to charge into reserve funds.

It also requires good co-ordination between technical and finance staff to ensure that charges are reduced when actual costs of individual items are less than the original estimate.

Under s42A of the Landlord and Tenant Act 1987 as added by s156 of the Commonhold and Leasehold Reform Act 2002, service charge contributions must be held in a separate trust account, and the leaseholder has the right to inspect the documents which show that this provision has been complied with.

A new s42B provides that failure to comply with the provision for service charge funds to be held in a separate trust account is a criminal offence.

The provisions of s42 do not apply to local authorities and registered social landlords.

❏ 5.14 Management fees and administration charges

The level of management fees (sometimes mistakenly called administration fees) that a landlord can charge is governed by three things, listed here in order of importance:

1. The provisions in the lease for fee calculation methods and for individual fees for particular activities

2. The reasonableness of the fees as required by legislation
3. The landlord's actual management and administration costs

Some leases do not contain specific provisions governing the level or method of calculating management fees. Many housing association and local authority leases do contain such a provision and it is usually a simple percentage of the direct service costs. There may also be a separate lease provision that governs the management or administration fees that can be added to major works costs, usually the same percentage used for the management fee.

It should be noted that both the RICS and ARHM Codes take the view that it is not good practice to use percentages unless the lease specifically requires it.

Reasonableness means that costs are both reasonable, and have been reasonably incurred – that is, the work was necessary and carried out at a reasonable cost.

The management fees charged by registered housing associations on leasehold schemes for the elderly are subject to limits published annually by the Housing Corporation, where such a limit is referred to in the lease.

The fixed percentages given in many RTB leases are generally in the range of 10% to 20% of direct service charges, which often does not meet the actual costs of leasehold management. This means that unless the landlord can vary the lease by agreement with leaseholders, which is difficult to achieve, the landlord must either subsidise leasehold management costs from its other budgets, or reduce service levels and therefore costs.

Reducing service levels materially may be difficult given the landlord's legal obligations and the fact that some estates may have a mixture of rented and leased homes.

The majority of local authority landlords simply absorb the shortfall, while others attempt to recover more through a variety of means. For example, one landlord may negotiate an additional fee under a management agreement that reflects the actual level of service that residents want, rather than the lower level of service that the management fee given in the lease could support. Such an arrangement on its own will not be legally binding or sufficient to sustain legal proceedings to recover arrears of service charges.

The ARHM Code of Practice lists management services, the costs of which can generally be considered as part of the management fee, subject always to the test of reasonableness. The RICS Code also provides guidance.

The inability to recoup the full costs of management has led to an increasing tendency to make a basic management charge that complies with the lease, and to make additional administration charges for undertaking particular tasks such as dealing with a solicitor's letter or responding to a leaseholder's mortgagor. More recently tasks such as sending an arrears letter or making a visit in connection with a breach of the lease have been added to the list of management tasks being charged for outside of the basic management fee. After all, why should the costs of such an enquiry fall upon other leaseholders in the block that are not in arrears or selling?

St Mary's Mansions Ltd v Limegate Investment Co Ltd, Sarruf & others QBD [13 November 2002] TLR CA

A long lease contained provisions that entitled the landlord to recover *"the costs of all other services which the lessor may at its absolute discretion provide"* and for the *"reasonable and proper fees"* for general management of the building.

The Court of Appeal held that these did not, on a proper construction of the lease, entitle the lessor to include its legal costs of proceedings for arrears of charges and ground rent as part of the lessee's service charge.

There has been evidence of abuse by some landlords as a result of which s158 and Schedule 11 of the Commonhold and Leasehold Reform Act 2002 have been drafted to bring some control over these practices. The Act defines an administration charge as an amount payable in connection with:

- Applications or the granting of approvals under the lease, such as assignments, subletting, improvements, keeping pets
- The provision of information or documents under the lease, such as insurance documents or service costs invoices
- Failure by the leaseholder to make a payment due to the landlord
- Arising from a breach of the lease by the leaseholder

There are two types of administration charge; variable charges and those specified in leases as either a fixed sum or as a calculation formula.

Leaseholders have the right to challenge the reasonableness of variable charges at an LVT, however the LVT would have to be asked to vary the lease by the leaseholder or landlord where a charge is specified in the lease.

In respect of either type of administration charge the LVT has new powers, as it has for service charges, to look beyond just reasonableness. Leaseholders in future will be able to ask a LVT to decide if a charge is payable, when, to whom, by whom and the manner in which it is payable.

These powers of the LVT apply whether the leaseholder has already paid the charge or not.

Any invoice or demand must be accompanied by a summary of the leaseholder's rights about the charges. A prescribed form of words is to be issued by the ODPM in mid 2004.

These are matters that may therefore be charged for outside the management fee component of the annual service charge.

Landlords should make it clear to leaseholders what is included within the management fee and therefore included in the annual service charge, and what matters will be the subject of separate administration charges should they arise. A menu of potential administration charges should be available to leaseholders.

A landlord or managing agent may be responsible for managing leaseholders with different leases and therefore it may not be able to apply a common approach to the composition of the management fee across all leasehold properties managed.

❑ 5.15 Service charges for newly built or refurbished homes

Service charges should be considered at the scheme feasibility stage when the size, type, design and future management of the development will be decided together with its financial viability based on the rents and service charges, and, where appropriate, anticipated sales proceeds.

The detailed design of the scheme will impact on service charge costs for the life of the scheme, so it is one of the most important and often neglected aspects of scheme design. An estimated service charge calculation should form part of the feasibility of the scheme and should be reviewed at the scheme approval stage.

Proposed leases and freehold covenants and tenancy agreements need to be checked to clarify what cannot be charged for.

An overall service charge policy should be developed that can be applied to all developments with a procedure for review in situations where the costs appear to be high and do not produce sustainable service charges.

Block costs are charged to residents of a particular block. Estate costs, where there is more than one block, are charged in proportion to the number of homes on the estate.

Service charge matters to consider at the scheme design stage

Estates

- CCTV system – can be costly – consider whether running costs (and depreciation) to be borne by service charges – decide within policy
- Car parking areas, location, security, lighting – automatic barriers have to be maintained
- Lighting of areas not 'attached' to a block – including robust practical lighting systems
- Grounds maintenance of communal areas which are not 'attached' to a block
- Go for long term good quality provision of hard and soft landscaping – think through private v public space
- Make sure any tree works are carried out as part of the capital costs of the scheme
- Consider persuading local authority to adopt roads and street lighting – design and build to adoptable standards
- Water supplies and sewerage to be provided to adoptable standards to allow for later adoption, if there are technicalities preventing adoption at the outset
- Concierge/estate management staffing, duties and accommodation – think it through – how are the revenue costs to be paid for
- Play areas – pros and cons – who pays for insurance, regular inspection, repairs, replacements etc
- Examine secure by design issues

Blocks

- Cleaning of entrance halls, lobbies, corridors, stairs – floors and walls and communal windows and doors and light fittings
- Floor coverings – type, anticipated life, cleaning method and frequency
- Quality and durability of finish and appearance
- Avoid creating areas which are awkward or difficult to clean without special equipment and skills
- Windows and any glazed areas must be cleanable – ideally from inside
- Communal electricity costs – for internal lighting, lift if any, landlord power supply for cleaning machines etc
- Communal electricity costs for external lighting – design and metering – block costs should be separate from estate costs if there are a number of blocks and especially if they are of different design
- Door entry systems – capital cost to be depreciated – service contract for call outs and repairs or provide through general maintenance service if expertise available. Repairs are generally chargeable to service charges. Use known products that are robust and easy to repair/replace. Consider the access for trades people.

- CCTV system – can be costly – consider whether running costs (and depreciation) to be borne by service charges – decide within policy
- Lifts – capital cost to be depreciated – service contract required – for call outs and repairs – telephone line and calls costs for lift – decide whether all costs are to be charged to service charges. Consider design to minimise lift running costs – ie small block of flats with 4 floors and 7 or 8 flats requires a lift
- Communal water supply for block – consider pros and cons – costs usually include a water meter for supply and sewage costs
- Communal drying areas – eg rotary driers – provision and repair and maintenance can be a service charge item
- Rubbish collection and storage – allow space for future expansion and recycling facilities – check local authority requirements and future intentions. Consider eurobins v paladins. Decide whether to provide the bins as part of capital costs (therefore depreciate) or to hire them. Cleaning of bins – may be included in hire costs. Repair of owned bins is a chargeable cost
- Consideration of innovative impacting systems for rubbish
- Fire detection/fighting systems – many need regular, recorded monitoring, responding to alarms – how are these going to be managed?

❑ 5.16 Further reading on service charges

Association of Retirement Housing Managers (1996 – revised edition due spring 2004) *Code of Practice for Private Sheltered Housing*   ISBN 0 952699 0 2
Statutory approval given under s87 Leasehold Reform, Housing and Urban Development Act 1993

Royal Institution of Chartered Surveyors (1997 – revised edition in progress) *Service Charge Residential Management Code* ISBN 0 85406 643 8
Statutory approval given under s87 Leasehold Reform, Housing and Urban Development Act 1993

Rawson, Derek (2003) *Service Charges – A Guide for Registered Social Landlords* National Housing Federation

Freedman, Philip, Shapiro, Eric & Slater, Brian (2002, 3rd edition) *Service Charges, Law and Practice* Jordan Publishing Ltd ISBN 0 85308 710 5

Housing Corporation (2003) *A Charter for Housing Association Applicants and Residents*

Cox, Nigel (1993, 4th edition expected 2004) *Running a Flat Management Company* Jordan Publishing Ltd ISBN 0 85308 8608

Broomleigh Housing Association *Your service charges explained* – useful 21 page booklet for Broomleigh leaseholders
www.broomleigh.org.uk

Housing Corporation *Circular 01/03* on right to a service charge loan
www.housingcorp.gov.uk

Further guidance on service charges will be available from the Housing Corporation in 2004.

CHAPTER 6

SERVICE CHARGES FOR MAJOR WORKS AND IMPROVEMENTS

This chapter explains the difference between repairs and improvements and examines some of the harder-to-define areas of responsibility for meeting the costs of improvement work.

It considers the particular difficulties for landlords and leaseholders affected by major regeneration schemes, and explains the options for providing financial and other assistance to leaseholders faced with large service charge bills as a result.

Consultation in respect of major works and improvements is dealt with in Chapter 7.

❑ 6.1 The difference between repairs and improvements

Nothing in leases or legislation guides a landlord in the definition of what constitutes a repair or improvement. The definition is governed by case law and the interpretation of the courts, and this is often contradictory. In general terms, the courts have tended to interpret an improvement to be works which amount to the provision of something different in nature from that which was originally provided under the lease, rather than the mere maintenance of the building. This has not ruled out using modern materials, but the finished repair or renewal should be of a similar standard to the original. However the Lands Tribunal case *LB Wandsworth v Griffin [2000]* has moved away from this approach, and is helpful in that it set out the factors that should be established in considering whether works go beyond mere 'repair'.

The case considered elements of work to the block in which the flat was situated including the replacement of metal windows with UPVC double glazed units and the replacement of a flat roof to the block with a pitched roof.

The Tribunal agreed that the landlord's approach of valuing the works over their expected lifetime and discounting the hypothetical cost of future repairs was reasonable, even though in the case of the pitched roof, no financial advantage could be shown for the first forty years. The Tribunal concluded that both the window renewal and the pitched replacement roof could be regarded as a repair if they were cheaper in the long run.

The Tribunal ruled that the landlord must take the following factors into account:
- The nature of the building
- The nature and extent of the defects to be remedied
- The nature, extent and cost of the proposed remedial works together with any alternatives
- The value of the building and its expected lifespan
- The effect of the works and the value and lifespan of the building
- Current building practice

The landlord must therefore properly consider these things and come to a reasonable conclusion, if it is to be able to withstand a challenge from a leaseholder on its right to charge.

Each set of circumstances will be different and must be assessed on its own merits in the light of the most recent case law. If there is any doubt legal advice should be sought.

■ Improvement contributions

For homes sold under the Right to Buy, an amendment to s125 of the Housing Act 1985, contained in s4(2) of the Housing and Planning Act 1986 introduced the concept of "improvement contributions" and enables a landlord to recover the costs of improvements as long as provision is made to do so under the terms of the lease.

See the Table on pages 93-94 for differences between repairs and improvements.

■ Consultation on improvement works

Consultation on improvement works was not required under s20. However, the Commonhold and Leasehold Reform Act 2002 has now extended the definition of a service charge to include works of improvement so that consultation on any *"qualifying works"* – that is works resulting in a charge to an individual leaseholder in excess of £250, whether a repair or an improvement, will be subject to the consultation requirements under the Act and contained in the Service Charges (Consultation Requirements) (England) Regulations (SI 2003 No 1987).

Differences between repairs and improvements

This is intended as a general guide not a definitive list.

Repairs	Improvements
External decorations	
Internal decorations to communal areas	
Repairing or replacing existing flooring in communal areas. Laying a tiled floor for the first time over an existing concrete floor or replacing the current flooring material with one of a higher standard for health and safety reasons	Replacing an existing flooring to a higher standard using more expensive materials where it is not possible to show any cost saving over the life of the new flooring under the principals established in *LB Wandsworth v Griffin* (see Chapter 6.1 above)
Renewal of gutters and down pipes	
Renewal of plumbing such as cold water storage tanks	
Renewal of flat/pitched roof involving repair and replacement with roof of a similar construction to current standards. Replacement to an improved specification eg renewing a flat roof with a pitched roof where it can be shown that over the life of the new roof this will result in a cost saving on renewing the roof as existing but to current standards	Renewing a flat roof with a pitched roof where it is not possible to show any cost saving over the life of the new pitched roof in comparison with replacing as existing but to current standards
Replacement of windows with the same or similar including the replacement with single glazing even if different materials are used, and replacement to an improved specification eg double glazing where it can be shown that over the life of the new windows it will result in a cost saving on renewing the windows as existing	Replacement of windows to an improved specification where it is not possible to show any cost saving over the life of the new windows in comparison with replacing as existing but to current standards
Replacement of doors to the same standard	Replacement of doors to an improved specification unless this can be shown as reasonable in producing a cost saving over the expected life of the new door
Resurfacing of roads or footpaths	Redesigning external areas eg creating new parking areas or play areas

Repairs	Improvements
Renewing fences and walls with the same or similar materials or renewal to an improved specification where it can be shown that over the life of the new fence this will result in a cost saving on renewing the fence as existing (see Chapter 6.1 above)	Renewing fences and walls with improved materials eg three strand wire replaced with brick wall or close boarded fence unless this can be shown to produce a cost saving over the expected life of the new fence
Repair to cladding or brickwork	Recladding to improve insulation
Replacement of damaged or defective loft insulation	Increasing loft insulation to improve thermal efficiency or the provision of new energy efficiency measures eg cavity wall insulation. Grants may be available to assist the leaseholder with the costs.
Replacement of TV aerial	Provision of TV aerial or replacement of existing TV aerial with access to satellite or more channels
Repairs of existing lifts or renewal as existing to current standards or renewal to an improved specification if it can be shown that over the life of the new lift this will be a cost saving on renewing the lift as existing but to current standards	First time installation of a lift. Renewals of lifts where the design and construction changes and upgrades the nature of the lift system unless this can be shown as reasonable in producing a cost saving over the expected life of the new lift
Repairs to existing door entry systems/communal doors or renewal as existing but to current standard	First time installation of door entry systems including the replacement of communal doors to facilitate the installation. Renewals where the design and construction changes and upgrades the nature of the system unless this can be shown as reasonable in producing a cost saving over the expected life of the new door entry system
Repairs to existing refuse chutes and bin stores or renewal as existing but to current standards	First time installation of refuse systems. Renewals where the design and construction changes and upgrades the type of system unless this can be shown as reasonable in producing a cost saving over the expected life of the new system

❑ 6.2 Responsibility for repairs

The responsibility for repairs to leasehold property is split between the leaseholder and the landlord. Each party's repairing obligations are usually set out in schedules or clauses in the lease. Leases vary widely in the level of detail in which repairing obligations are defined.

■ Typical repairing obligations of leaseholders

Leases will usually require the leaseholder to keep the property in good repair and condition (including fixtures and fittings). This means the property should be maintained at a reasonable standard for a home of its type and age. Where items are worn out the leaseholder is expected to replace them, and if necessary to undertake some rebuilding to keep the property in repair.

Leaseholders will generally be responsible for:

- Windows, window fastenings and glazing (but not window frames attached to the structure
- The ceilings (but not joists or beams)
- Floor boards and screeds, but not joists or floor slabs
- Interior plaster or other surfaces of the ceiling and exterior walls of the dwelling
- Interior non structural walls
- The entrance door(s) and door fastenings (but not the door frame), internal doors, frames and fastenings
- Tanks/cisterns*
- Pipes, wiring, cables and conduits supplying water, electricity and gas*
- Pipes, guttering, drains and sewers removing waste water and sewerage*
- Anything installed for the supply of central heating and hot water*
- Fixtures and fittings eg bath, WC, gas fire, fireplace, kitchen units etc
- Plaster work and internal decoration

* The leaseholder is responsible for these things inside or outside the flat if they serve only the leaseholder's property.

■ Typical repairing responsibilities of landlords

Leases will usually require that the landlord must keep the items listed below in good repair and condition. This again means they must be maintained at a reasonable standard for the age and type of property and that where items are worn out they can be replaced and where necessary the landlord can undertake rebuilding to keep the property in repair.

Landlords are generally responsible for:

- The main structure of the property including
    - the structure of all walls and floors forming the external boundary of the dwelling
    - the foundations
    - the whole roof structure including the roof space and chimneys
    - door and window frames in the external walls
    - internal structural walls
    - balconies
    - any walls fences or gates to the building
- The services to the building including
    - communal pipes, wiring, and conduits supplying water, electricity and gas
    - communal tanks/cisterns
    - rain water pipes, guttering, and main drains
    - refuse chutes
    - lifts
    - communal heating systems
- The common parts of the building including
    - staircases, passages and landings all the internal parts of the building including any apparatus or fixtures and fittings.
    - internal and external redecorations
- The common parts of the surrounding estate
    - Baggage stores, garages and parking spaces including locking posts and door frames (but excluding doors and windows)
    - External communal areas including trees, lawns, walls, fences, paths roadways and lighting etc

Note: It is essential to check the precise repairing obligations of individual leases and to make sure that leasehold management staff and other staff responsible for receiving repairs requests and issuing repairs orders are fully aware of the boundaries of responsibility of each party to the leases.

■ Work where responsibility may be difficult to establish
Windows and double-glazing
In many leases window frames and catches are the landlord's responsibility, whilst glazing to individual flats is the leaseholder's responsibility. Whilst this is a straightforward division of responsibility, there are particular concerns involving double glazing where responsibility is more difficult to establish:

1. **Where glazing in a UPVC frame fails, and it is initially impossible to decide if this is a fault with the glazed unit (leaseholder's responsibility) or a failure of how it is sealed into the frame (the landlord's responsibility).**

Inspection may be needed before responsibility can be clearly established. Generally if the glazing shows signs of condensation or water penetration between the glass panels it is likely to be the glazed unit that has failed and the leaseholder is responsible for replacing it. If, however water is penetrating around the glass there may be a fault with the seals in the frame itself. Where, upon inspection, the fault is found to be with the glazing and therefore the leaseholder's responsibility, the landlord should charge them with the cost of the inspection.

2. **Where the leaseholder has replaced the catches or other fixings and they become defective.**
   As the catches are the landlord's responsibility, the leaseholder should have sought permission to replace them. However even though the leaseholder has replaced them they are still the landlord's responsibility. The landlord should carry out the work but the cost of replacement or repair should be recharged to the leaseholder.

3. **Where the installation is still under the manufacturer's guarantee.**
   Leaseholders should be charged with the costs to the landlord of repairing or replacing frames that have become defective, but are still under guarantee, as the landlord is the beneficiary of the guarantee, not the leaseholder. If a successful claim is subsequently made under the guarantee, then the leaseholder(s) service charge account should be credited with the amount claimed.

4. **Where leaseholders wish to replace their own windows.**
   Whilst private sector landlords generally will not allow leaseholders to do this, most social landlords normally will agree to the windows being installed to a specification agreed by the landlord, and any local planning or building control requirements being met. If a leaseholder seeks permission to renew their windows, a check should be made to see if the landlord has included the block in a future window renewal programme, and the leaseholder advised of this. They should be told that if they do renew their windows, they will still have to meet their proportion of the costs of renewing the windows to the remainder of the block.

   When a window renewal scheme is planned leaseholders should be consulted in the normal manner under s20, but should be told that even if they refuse to have the new windows, they will still have to meet their proportion of the total cost of renewing the remaining windows (see *Broomleigh v Hughes, High Court [1999]* explained in detail in Chapter 9.3).

Conservatories or other extensions attached to the structure

Conservatories and other extensions that are attached to the structure become part of that structure and therefore the landlord's responsibility to repair.

The landlord can avoid this by granting permission to the addition, subject to the costs of its future maintenance being met by the leaseholder. However, this will not extend to future leaseholders upon assignment. To ensure that maintenance responsibility remains with the leaseholder on assignment the landlord must formally grant a licence and ensure a record of this is kept.

The leaseholder should be asked to meet the landlord's fees and reasonable costs in granting the licence.

❑ 6.3 Paying for repairs

The landlord is able to reclaim from leaseholders a share of the costs of carrying out the landlord's repairing obligations, if the lease provides for this. However if the landlord carries out a repair that is the leaseholder's responsibility this cannot be charged to the leaseholder, unless it has been done because the leaseholder breached their own repairing obligations. When arranging major works contracts, items that are the leaseholder's responsibility should be excluded unless a separate enforceable agreement is reached with the leaseholder to pay for the work.

The landlord's responsibility under the lease may only be for repair and maintenance of the property. In these circumstances the costs of maintenance work that represents an improvement rather than a repair cannot generally be recovered from leaseholders. There will be situations, especially in major works contracts, where a desirable scheme will involve improvement and it will not be possible to exclude leaseholders as the work is to benefit the building and all its residents as a whole not just the individual leaseholder's home eg environmental improvements. The definition of repairs and improvements is considered in more detail in Chapter 6.2.

Managers in the social sector must also be aware of any undertakings given to leaseholders as part of any transfers of housing stock. Some stock transfer arrangements include, for example, guarantees that leaseholders would receive new UPVC double glazed windows, at no cost to themselves, as part of the regeneration strategy.

■ The boundaries of the leaseholder's property

The leaseholder's responsibility under the lease covers the property they have purchased and any services and drainage which serves only that property. It is important when assessing who is responsible for meeting the cost of a repair to understand the physical boundary to the leaseholder's property, and what may be included or excluded. This will be described in the lease, or in a schedule to the lease.

As a general rule, in the case of a leasehold flat, the property will extend:

- From the floor to the ceiling (but not the joists beams or floors, to which the ceiling is attached), and include

- The interior plaster, tiling and other surfaces where they attach to any floors ceilings or walls which form the boundary of the property.

The property will also include:

- Services and drainage systems if they only serve the flat even though they may be located outside that property.

Roof spaces above the property are not generally included in the leaseholder's property. The leaseholder may have a right of access to maintain services that supply only their property.

Most leases do not make specific reference to insulation in the roof space, but in general as the insulation provides a benefit to more than one property and is located in an area that is not included in an individual lease, then it is likely to be the responsibility of the landlord.

If it is unclear whether a repair falls within a leaseholder's property then consulting the repairing obligations of the leaseholder or those of the landlord as prescribed in the lease may help.

❏ 6.4 Leaseholders and regeneration schemes

The rapid growth in regeneration activity by both local authorities and housing associations in urban areas in recent years has created particular difficulties for leaseholders, mainly those who bought under the Right to Buy, or upon the subsequent resale of those properties.

Landlord and Tenant legislation was primarily designed for a private sector in which landlords are required to do no more than maintain property in accordance with the basic repairing obligations of leases. The legislation did not envisage social landlords embarking on massive and costly neighbourhood regeneration schemes to which leaseholders would be obliged to contribute.

The impact of the Decent Homes Standard will also lead to an acceleration in programmes of work to the blocks in which leaseholders live, and to works that are designed to provide longer-lasting and possibly more costly solutions, at least in the short term.

The majority of Right to Buy sales took place during a period when local authorities were not able to fund works that went beyond basic repair and improvement, and neither the staff advising potential purchasers nor the purchasers themselves foresaw the change in the financial climate that has enabled a rapid expansion of programmes to address wider aspects of neighbourhood renewal.

The impact of regeneration schemes on leaseholders differs significantly according to:

1. What their lease allows their landlord to charge for
2. How the works are being funded
3. Who their landlord is – local authority, traditional housing association or transfer association
4. The value of the property concerned and its locality
5. How the landlord defines repairs and improvements
6. How their landlord interprets "reasonableness"
7. How their landlord uses its discretionary powers

The range of variation these factors produce is vast, and means that for similar schemes undertaken by different public sector landlords, individual leaseholders can be treated quite differently and may be asked to pay absolutely nothing (because the stock transfer agreement and business plan was founded upon that assumption) or tens of thousands of pounds (because the landlord chooses to use the full extent of its legal powers to recover costs).

The current discretionary powers to assist only those leaseholders facing severe hardship are inadequate, as even households with reasonable incomes will have problems when faced with service charge bills amounting to tens of thousands of pounds, and what constitutes severe hardship is left to individual landlords to decide.

Local authorities' wider fiduciary duties restrict their capacity to waive and reduce charges to leaseholders. Forgoing income to which an authority has a legal entitlement results in an increased burden to public finances either locally or nationally, and is therefore not permissible unless explicitly provided for in legislation or regulation.

All housing associations have to operate within the boundaries of their budgets and business plans, and charitable housing associations cannot freely forgo income to which they are entitled. Within these confines, however, associations can often devise measures that offer greater financial support to leaseholders affected by major regeneration proposals.

■ Some possible approaches to managing regeneration schemes that include leaseholders

At a very early stage in planning the scheme, and before beginning resident consultation, landlords need to consider the potential impact on leaseholders and prepare answers to the questions that leaseholders will raise. Whilst leaseholders and other tenants will have a common interest in seeing their estates improved, leaseholders will have to pay directly for much of the work undertaken and therefore will have different expectations from the consultation once it begins.

The landlord should consider:

What financial impact will the choices offered in the consultation exercise have on leaseholders?
Some options may include environmental and landscaping improvements, some elements of which may relate to estate security, which might be rechargeable, rather than to improving the appearance of the grounds, which may not be rechargeable. Increasing the size of bin chambers to accommodate larger bins may be chargeable, whilst another option of installing a modern underground collection system may not.

Which works will require leaseholders to contribute in full, in part or not at all?
In part this will be driven by terms of each lease, but there are other considerations – for example, a comprehensive regeneration scheme may involve replacing building components to which works of repair have only recently been carried out and for which leaseholders were charged. The landlord must decide if it is reasonable in those circumstances to charge leaseholders with the full cost of the new works. Similarly works that are being undertaken to improve community safety may be regarded by leaseholders as non-essential to the repair and upkeep of the estate. Landlords will need to demonstrate that those works will have a long-term financial benefit, for example in terms of reduced vandalism costs.

What forms of financial assistance could be made available to leaseholders?
It is not in the wider community's interest to allow a situation to arise in which leaseholders are more likely to default on their mortgages or service charges, and risk losing their homes through repossession. The landlord should offer a range of forms of assistance to leaseholders facing large service charge bills or, in the case of demolition, who are unable to find another suitable property in the area on the open market at an equivalent price.

It may also include other tenure options of shared ownership or returning to becoming a rent-paying tenant.

If internal refurbishment of tenanted homes requires temporary rehousing of tenants, how will leaseholders be treated?
The security of a handful of leaseholders left in a large otherwise empty block and the noise created as a result of major refurbishments works will be of concern to leaseholders and the landlord will need to plan their response.

If a demolition option is being offered to residents
What help would the landlord be able to offer to leaseholders that were unable to find another suitable property in the area on the open market at an equivalent price, and how would they be recompensed for their costs involved?

Could the redevelopment include suitable new homes either for shared ownership or outright sale that could be available for current leaseholders?

In deciding whether it is appropriate to charge leaseholders for all or part of the costs of individual components of regeneration schemes it will be helpful to consider the following:

1. The extent to which the scheme component contributes to the effective management or maintenance of the estate
2. The extent to which it contributes to the security of the estate
3. The extent to which the scheme component contributes purely to the appearance of the estate
4. Whether the scheme component has already been the subject of improvement/repair recently and charged to leaseholders (say within past five years)

■ The powers available to local authorities and housing associations under the Housing Act 1996

Directions issued under s219 and s220 of the Housing Act 1996 require local authorities, housing associations, Housing Action Trusts and Urban Development Corporations to limit charges for repair, maintenance or improvement works carried out with assistance from Estate Action, City Challenge, Single Regeneration Budget, the Estates Renewal Challenge Fund, the New Deal for Communities or the Private Finance Initiative.

The Direction also gave local authorities, housing associations, Housing Action Trusts and Urban Development Corporations *discretionary powers* to assist leaseholders faced with large service charge bills in addition to the mandatory requirements.

■ The scope of discretionary powers to financially assist leaseholders

Paragraph 6 of the Direction sets out the criteria that the landlord should take into account in deciding whether to waive or reduce the service charge. They are a mixture of matters that could lead to a view that a reduction would be reasonable, or not reasonable.

All the following criteria should be considered.

(a) *Any estimate of the costs of the works of repair, maintenance or improvement notified to the lessee or any predecessor in title before his or their purchase of the lease of the dwelling;*
   This means that if the service charge to be made is significantly greater than any estimate given previously to the current or a former leaseholder, the landlord could consider this to be a reason to reduce the charge.

(b) *Whether the purchase price paid by the lessee took account of the costs of the works of repair, maintenance or improvement;*
This means that if the purchase price paid by the leaseholder was a fair reflection of the condition of the property, building or estate – ie it would have been a higher price if the works for which a charge is now being made had already been carried out – then the landlord could consider this a reason not to reduce the charge.

(c) *Any benefit which a social landlord considers the lessee has received or will receive as a result of the works of repair, maintenance or improvement including an increase in the value of the lease (including reduction in the negative value of the lease), an increase in the energy efficiency of the dwelling, and an improvement in services or facilities;*
This means that if the leaseholder is going to benefit financially through an increase in value of the property, a reduction in outgoings, or an improvement in services then the landlord should take the value of that into account in deciding if it would be reasonable to make a reduction in the service charge.

(d) *Whether, upon receipt of an application by a lessee, a social landlord, having regard to the criteria set out in paragraph 7, considers that the lessee would suffer exceptional hardship in paying the service charge;*
This is the specific power to make a reduction if hardship is going to be experienced by the leaseholders as a result of the level of service charges, and it comes with its own set of criteria set out below.

The criteria for consideration in respect to exceptional hardship are set out in paragraph 7 of the Directions as follows:

(a) Whether the dwelling is the lessee's only or principal home;

(b) The total amount of the service charges which have been paid or are payable by the lessee since the lessee's purchase of the lease of the dwelling;

(c) The amount of the service charge payable in the year in which the lessee applies for a reduction because of exceptional hardship;

(d) The financial resources available to the lessee;

(e) The ability of the lessee to raise funds to pay the service charge;

(f) The ability of the lessee to pay the service charge if the social landlord were to extend the period for payment; and

(g) Any other circumstance of the lessee which the social landlord considers relevant.

It can be argued that items (a) to (c) provide landlords with the power to reduce or waive services charges regardless of any hardship that may be being experienced as a result of the level of charges; however, it is difficult to separate the two entirely as local authority landlords must also weigh up the balance of their duties to council tax payers and rent payers alongside their obligations, legal or otherwise, to leaseholders.

It means that unless the landlord can be convinced of hardship resulting from matters falling within items (a) to (c) it is unlikely to want to use its discretionary powers under these other criteria to make service charge reductions.

In practice this would require:

- The landlord to agree detailed rules for interpreting the criteria
- Finalised details and costs of the work to carried out to the estate
- An individual detailed examination by the landlord of the financial circumstances of each leaseholder

None of this affects the landlord's obligations under s20 of the Landlord and Tenant Act to consult the leaseholders' association on the detailed specification of works and the selection of contractors, and to consult both the association and individual leaseholders on the tenders subsequently received for the work.

■ The effect of lease provisions on regeneration proposals

Staff involved in scheme design must always take account of lease provisions that may be breached by features of the proposed regeneration scheme. For example, creating private gardens for ground floor flats from communal areas over which leaseholders have access rights may require leases to be varied, and leaseholders may not agree to this. Similarly, altering paths and access points may have clear community safety benefits, but if they result in breaches of the landlord's obligations under the lease, they cannot proceed until the lease has been suitably amended. Proceeding in breach could have very costly consequences if a leaseholder subsequently required the landlord to remedy its breach.

Relevant factors

There is no government guidance to landlords undertaking regeneration work in respect of the leaseholders living within the estates affected. In its absence, landlords should take the following factors into account:

- Landlord and tenant legislation was primarily designed for a private sector in which landlords are required to do no more than maintain property in accordance with the basic repairing obligations of leases. The legislation did not envisage social landlords embarking on massive and costly neighbourhood regeneration schemes that leaseholders would then have to pay for.

→

- The majority of Right to Buy sales took place during a period when councils were not able to fund works that went beyond basic repair and improvement, so neither the staff advising potential purchasers nor the purchasers themselves foresaw the change in the financial climate that has enabled a rapid acceleration of investment in social housing.
- Even households with reasonable incomes will have problems when faced with service charge bills amounting to tens of thousands of pounds.
- Many leaseholders will have low incomes and little further borrowing potential, but there will be a range of household economic situations, and the landlord similarly needs a range of forms of financial and other assistance to offer.
- The relationship of the increase in capital value of the leaseholders asset, and the costs the leaseholder must pay for major works is an important one. The property may have a future increased value, but it does not provide the immediate liquidity the leaseholder needs to pay for major works.
- It is not in the wider community's interest to create a situation in which leaseholders are more likely to default on their mortgages or service charges, and risk losing their homes through repossession.
- The problem will not go away – in fact it will increase with every subsequent regeneration scheme that proceeds.

These are the factors that it is reasonable for local authority and housing association landlords to weigh against any additional financial burden that they believe may be created for the rest of the community as a result of financially assisting leaseholders.

Potentially landlords can:

1. Provide the mandatory reductions of service charges in the Directions issued under the Housing Act 1996, but this will depend on the precise source of funding for the works. See Chapter 9.1 for details of the Directions.
2. Provide a scheme for discretionary reductions in line with the Directions under the Act, taking into account the circumstances of individual households and the wider impact of the costs of such a scheme, and any factors such as those mentioned earlier. It will need to be flexible.
3. Provide interest free or low interest loans.
4. Provide extended repayment periods.
5. Operate some form of shared equity scheme (local authorities will have to work with a partner housing association) to enable the release of some equity in the property to pay for major works.
6. Buy back the property either directly or through a partner housing association.

7. Put a charge on the property to recoup costs on subsequent sale.

8. Assist with relocation costs – not usually the main concern with leaseholders, although every little helps.

9. Allowing the leaseholder to become a tenant again is a theoretical possibility. The Right to Buy would be created again after two years, but any discount previously received would have to be deducted from any future discount entitlement. The RTB would not exist if the tenancy offered was a an assured tenancy. However this option is likely to be extremely unpopular with leaseholders, and a much better option is that of moving to a shared ownership/flexible tenure arrangement.

Regeneration schemes case study

In both cases leaseholders are faced with either radical refurbishment or demolition and redevelopment.

In Case A, the property values are low, and the homes were transferred to a housing association to enable the proposals to be funded.

In Case B, the property values are high, and the council intends to undertake the works itself.

The implications for leaseholders in Case A are that demolition and redevelopment is unsatisfactory as the market values they will get for their homes will not enable them to purchase similar properties locally. On the other hand, radical refurbishment is a fantastic deal because, in this particular case, the council transferred the stock to the association with the promise to leaseholders that they would not have to pay for any structural or external works, and the association produced its business plan on that basis.

The implications for leaseholders in Case B are the reverse, as under a demolition and redevelopment option, they get relatively high prices for their homes, whilst the radical refurbishment option may hit them with bills of between £30,000 and £50,000 each.

In practice, in Case A the association is able to offer a range of buy back, alternative homes – and anything else that is needed to enable the chosen scheme to proceed, whilst in Case B the council is likely to shelter behind its wider fiduciary duties, and offer very little discretionary assistance to leaseholders, with the distinct possibility that no scheme at all proceeds in the case of demolition and redevelopment as the compulsory purchase process would be too prolonged.

Alternatively, if radical refurbishment becomes the chosen option, then the leaseholders have no prospect of being able to afford the bills they will get, and their homes are effectively blighted. The only sales they can make are to property management companies, which is exactly what has happened on some estates.

The other factor to consider here is that in neither case have leaseholders any real say in what will happen, as they comprise only a small minority of the residents concerned. Their value to the diversity of the community, both economically and socially on both estates is significant however. In many cases, the interests of both tenants and leaseholders should be the same, but because of the different financial impact that regeneration schemes have on them, they often pull in different directions.

❑ 6.5 Further reading on major works, improvements and repairing obligations

The Leasehold Advisory Service (LEASE) – an independent advice agency funded by government grant – various downloadable leaflets and information and guidance available including details of LVT decisions
www.lease-advice.org.uk

Wandsworth LBC v Griffin (2000) – Lands Tribunal decisions re repairs and improvements

The Association of Retirement Housing Managers (ARHM) – for Code of Practice, revised edition due spring 2004, also good practice notes for members
www.arhm.org

The Royal Institution of Chartered Surveyors (RICS) – professional organisation for Chartered Surveyors – produces Code of Practice for service charge residential management and other residential management information
www.rics.org.uk

Chapter 7

Consultation Requirements following the Commonhold and Leasehold Reform Act 2002

This chapter explains the requirements for consultation before undertaking major works of repair or improvement, or entering into long term contracts for the provision of services.

It explains the implications for local authorities, in particular those that are contemplating changes to housing management arrangements through ALMOs, PFI contracts and partnering arrangements.

❏ 7.1 Legal requirements

The Commonhold and Leasehold Reform Act 2002 introduces important changes to the requirements for consulting leaseholders, which are contained in regulations issued along with the Second Commencement Order of August 2003 (SI No 1986).

The Act allows the Secretary of State to make regulations excluding certain classes of agreement and to set the financial limits above which consultation will be required. These came into force on 31 October 2003 through the **Service Charges (Consultation Requirements) (England) Regulations 2003 (SI 2003 No 1987)**.

The regulations extend the requirement for consultation to contracts for all services, not just major works. They are complex and require very careful planning and administration, particularly by local authorities, which are the landlords most extensively affected by the regulations.

Put as simply as possible, there are two main categories of contract upon which consultation may be required:

- Qualifying works – such as major repairs and improvements, but may also be day-to-day repairs above the prescribed amount
- Qualifying long-term agreements (QLTAs) – such as management contracts and partnering arrangements

The complications occur when qualifying works are undertaken under qualifying long-term agreements, and when contracts have been let under EU procurement rules which themselves require public notice.

These requirements in respect of works under long-term agreements have been created to resolve the difficulties that partnering and PFI contracts have caused for leaseholder consultation. Landlords that had already entered into PFI and partnering contracts for works, before the commencement of these rules, will be able to use the procedure for major works under long term agreements. The position for landlords who wish to enter into PFI and partnering contract works after the commencement of the rules can be found in Chapter 7.3.

In order to deal with the range of circumstances that may occur, the regulations identify four categories of contract upon which consultation may be required, and the procedures to be followed in each case vary slightly. The detailed requirements are contained in four schedules to the regulations as follows:

- **Schedule 1** – *Qualifying long term agreements*, other than those for which public notice is required
- **Schedule 2** – *Qualifying long term agreements* for which public notice is required
- **Schedule 3** – *Qualifying works* under *qualifying long term agreements* including those QLTAs already entered into, or for which public notice was given prior to the commencement date of the regulations (31 October 2003)
- **Schedule 4**
  (Part 1) – *Qualifying works* for which public notice is required
  (Part 2) – *Qualifying works* for which public notice is not required

The regulations are new, complex, and, at the time of writing, untried in practice and in some cases the wording is capable of more than one interpretation. In the months following their publication best practice in their implementation will emerge and model procedures, forms and letters will be published. It is therefore essential that leasehold managers remain alert to this and do not rely entirely upon the initial interpretations published here.

There is no substitute for very careful reading of the regulations, but the key points to be aware of are set out on the following page.

Key points to note about the new section 20 consultation requirements

- There are now three separate procedures for major works rather than one

- Landlords that have already entered into PFI and partnering contracts for works, before the commencement of these rules, will be able to use the procedure for major works under long term agreements. They will find that, unlike previously, they are able to meet consultation rules. The position for landlords wishing to enter into PFI and partnering contracts after the commencement of the rules can be found in Chapter 7.3

- There are also sub-procedures for works or agreements that are let under EU procurement rules

- The prescribed amount for consultation on works to a building or other premises is now more than £250 including VAT per leaseholder

- The prescribed amount for long term agreements is more than £100 including VAT per leaseholder per annum

- The prescribed amounts are per leaseholder not per unit; it is therefore necessary to refer to the service charge proportions in the lease

- All leaseholders as well as recognised residents' associations have been given the right to nominate contractors in certain circumstances

- Leaseholders of local authorities and housing associations are not limited to nominating contractors from the approved list of that landlord

- Landlords do not have to consult separately with those who subsequently exercise their Right to Buy if the landlord has already completed consultation with everyone else

- Contracts between an ALMO and a local authority have been exempted

- Other agreements which are exempted are: contracts of employment; Tenant Management Organisations; holding companies and subsidiaries; subsidiaries of the same holding company. Also where the property is untenanted when an agreement of less than five years is entered into

- An element of reasonableness has been inserted into those provisions where the landlord can state a place and hours for inspection of documents. Copies can be requested free of charge

- Although the notices described in the procedure do not have to be sent to all leaseholders if it is possible to post notices that will come to their attention, in practice, as some leaseholders may be non-resident, notices really do need to be sent individually.

❑ 7.2 The procedures to be followed

■ For long term contracts – (Qualifying Long Term Agreements – no public notice required) (*Schedule 1*)

Summary of the procedure

Serve a Notice of Intention

↓

Allow 30 days for observations and nominations of contractor

↓

Obtain estimates

↓

Prepare landlord's proposals including summary/response to any observations made

↓

Serve Notice of Landlord's Proposals

↓

Allow 30 days for observations

↓

Enter into QLTA

↓

Serve Notice of Reasons including a response to any observations within 21 days of entering into agreement to all lessees and RTA (recognised residents' associations).

What are Qualifying Long Term Agreements (QLTAs)?

Amendments to s20 and the addition of s20ZA in the Landlord and Tenant Act 1985 have been made by the Commonhold and Leasehold Reform Act 2002 to introduce the concept of the *'Qualifying long term agreement'*.

Qualifying Long Term Agreements are agreements entered into, by or on behalf of the landlord or a superior landlord, for a term of more than 12 months – this can be for works or goods and services. Some stock management contracts and other partnering arrangements will fall within this definition.

Sections 20 and 20ZA apply to all categories of long term contract except employment contracts, for example of concierges, porters or wardens, although there are special arrangements for contracts that have previously been consulted upon or that have been entered into under EU Public Procurement rules (see later).

Tenant Management Organisations within the meaning of s27AB of the Housing Act 1985 are also excluded, as are agreements between associated companies, such as where the landlord contracts with a company in the same group to carry out the management of schemes as an agent.

Agreements with ALMOs are also exempted.

The new requirements apply to qualifying long-term agreements that result in a contribution exceeding £100 per annum including VAT being required from an individual leaseholder in any accounting period for which the agreement runs.

Two important points to note here are:
- **That landlords will have to estimate in advance the likely contribution of leaseholders over the whole period of the contract, and**
- **Where apportionments amongst leaseholders vary, it is the largest proportion to be paid that needs to be checked against the prescribed amount. If only one leaseholder's contribution exceeds the amount it will still be necessary to consult with all leaseholders.**

Managers will not have to consult on existing contracts entered into prior to the date of the Commencement Order rules even if such contract has more than 12 months to run. There will however have to be consultation when that contract is due for retendering.

If when the Qualifying Long Term Agreement is entered into there are no leaseholders affected by the agreement, as could be the case with a new development and the contract is for a term not exceeding five years, there is no requirement to consult during the period of the agreement.

Details of the procedure – Schedule 1

Stage 1   Landlord serves Notice of Intention on leaseholders and recognised residents' associations (RTA)
- Describes what the long-term agreement is for (ie what goods or services are to be provided or what works are to be carried out under the agreement) or specifies where details can be inspected
- States the landlord's reasons for wishing to enter into the agreement and, if works are involved under the agreement, why such works are necessary
- Invites written observations within 30 days of the date of the notice which have to be considered
- Invites leaseholders and RTA to nominate a contractor

Stage 2   Landlord considers observations before deciding to proceed

Stage 3   If deciding to proceed landlord seeks estimates

If an RTA nominates a contractor then the landlord shall try to obtain an estimate from that contractor.

If individual leaseholders nominate only one contractor then the landlord shall try to obtain an estimate from that contractor.

Where more than one contractor is nominated by leaseholders, the landlord must endeavour to obtain an estimate from the contractor receiving the most nominations.

In the event of a tie the landlord may decide which nominated contractor to approach.

Where individual leaseholders nominate a different contractor from the RTA, the landlord must endeavour to obtain estimates from both.

If leaseholders nominate a contractor who is not already on the landlord's approved list, the landlord will have to ask that contractor to make an application to be admitted to the approved list and provide guidance to enable them to qualify. If they do not apply, or fail to meet the reasonable criteria required by the landlord (which from a good practice point of view should be set out in the invitation to tender) then it seems likely that the landlord will have done all that they reasonably can and should award the contract to a contractor who meets their approved list and invitation to tender criteria.

Stage 4   Landlord prepares contract proposals
- Landlord has to prepare at least two proposals based on estimates received
- At least one shall be from a person unconnected with the landlord
- If an estimate is received from a nominee of leaseholder or RTA then a proposal must be prepared based on it
- Each proposal must contain a description of works/services under the agreement
- The name of the contractor and any connection with the landlord must be provided
- The duration of the agreement and any provisions for variation of the costs must be specified
- There must be an estimate of the leaseholder's contribution

(Where this is not possible an estimate of the total cost of the works to the whole premises must be given; where this is not possible a statement of the applicable unit cost or hourly/daily rate must be given)

If the landlord received observations in Stage 2 above, then each proposal must contain a summary of those observations and the landlord's response to them.

Stage 5   Landlord notifies each leaseholder and RTA of the proposals
- Either provides copy of each proposal to leaseholders/RTA or gives information where the proposals can be inspected
- Invites written observations within 30 days which must be considered

Stage 6   Landlord considers observations, makes a decision and enters into the agreement

Stage 7   Landlord gives reasons to leaseholders for having entered into the agreement within 21 days of the date of agreement
- The landlord has to write to all leaseholders and RTA or state where the information can be inspected
- The landlord must both state reasons for choosing the particular contractor and
- If any observations were received, provide a summary of them and the landlord's response to them
- The landlord need not give reasons or reply to observations in writing if either of the following occurs:
  - The contract is awarded to the nominated contractor
  - The contract went to the lowest tenderer

Variation to the basic procedure under Schedule 1 where the Qualifying Long Term Agreement is with a managing agent

As above, but at Stage 4 the proposals must include information on whether the proposed managing agents are members of a trade association or if they subscribe to any code of practice and the names of such association or code of practice.

Variation to the basic procedure for Qualifying Long Term Contracts for which Public Notice under EU procurement rules is required (eg Partnering Contracts – Schedule 2)

There is a simplified procedure for contracts that require Public Notice under EU Regulations, which only allows comments and observations to be made on the proposed works, not on the selection of a contractor:

Stage 1   Landlord serves Notice of Intention on leaseholders and RTA
- Describes what the long-term agreement is for or states where details can be inspected
- States the landlord's reasons for wishing to enter the agreement and, if works are involved, why the works are necessary
- States why the landlord is not inviting nominations of contractors ie because public notice is to be given
- Invites observations

Stage 2   Landlord has regard to observations and if he decides to go ahead prepares a proposal with
- The name of the proposed parties to the agreement and any connection they have to the landlord
- An estimate of the leaseholder's contribution
  (*Where this is not possible an estimate of the total cost of the works to the premises must be given; where this is not possible a statement of the*

applicable hourly/daily rate must be given). If none of these are possible then a statement of why not and the date by which the landlord expects to have the cost information available.

- If the landlord has received observations then the proposal must contain a summary of those observations and the landlord's response to them

Stage 3   Landlord gives all leaseholders and RTA a notice that he has prepared the proposal and either attaches the proposal or informs them where it can be inspected. The notice must invite written observations on the proposal within 30 days

Stage 4   Following notification of the proposal consideration has to be given to any observations and the landlord must give his response in writing to any observations, to the person(s) who sent them, within 21 days of their receipt

■ **For works above the prescribed amount (Qualifying Works) – to a building or other premises, where Public Notice under EU procurement rules is not required (*Schedule 4 – Part 2*)**

Summary of the procedure

Serve a Notice of Intention

Allow 30 days for observations on works and nominations of contractor

Obtain estimates

Issue a "Paragraph (B)" statement setting out estimated costs and summary/ responses to any observations made

and

Serve a Notice specifying where the estimates may be inspected and inviting observations

Allow 30 days for observations on estimates

Enter into major works contract

Serve Notice of Reasons and summary/responses to any observations to all leaseholders and RTAs within 21 days of entering into agreement.

Details of the procedure

Stage 1   Landlord serves Notice of Intention on all leaseholders and RTA
- Describes works to be carried out in general terms or specifies where more details can be inspected if it is a complex project
- States the landlord's reasons for considering it necessary to carry out the works
- Invites written observations within 30 days of date of notice, which have to be considered
- Invites any leaseholder and the RTA to nominate a contractor

Stage 2   Leaseholders have 30 days to reply
- Landlord considers observations before deciding to proceed to seek estimates

Stage 3   Landlord obtains at least two estimates including one from the leaseholders' nominees, if applicable (see note below)

It is also important to remember that:
- If an RTA nominates a contractor then the landlord must try to obtain an estimate
- If the leaseholders only nominate one contractor then the landlord shall try to obtain an estimate from that contractor
- Where more than one contractor is nominated by leaseholders, the landlord must endeavour to obtain an estimate from the contractor receiving the most nominations
- In the event of a tie the landlord may decide which nominated contractor to approach
- Where individual leaseholders nominate a different contractor from the RTA, the landlord must endeavour to obtain estimates from both

If leaseholders nominate a contractor who is not already on the landlord's approved list, the landlord will have to ask that contractor to make an application to be admitted to the approved list and provide guidance to enable them to qualify. If they do not apply, or fail to meet the reasonable criteria required by the landlord (which from a good practice point of view should be set out in the invitation to tender) then it seems likely that the landlord will have done all that they reasonably can and should award the contract to a contractor who meets their approved list and invitation to tender criteria.

These principles apply to public sector landlords, but also to private sector landlords and managing agents that operate reasonable approved list criteria.

Stage 4   'Paragraph B' Statement issued to leaseholders containing:
- At least 2 estimates of the costs of the proposed works (at least one must be from a contractor unconnected with the landlord)
- Details of where the detailed estimates may be inspected
- A summary of the observations made on the Notice of Intention
- Invite written observations of the estimates within 30 days, which must be considered

Stage 5   Consider observations received within 30 days of date of notice

Stage 6   Landlord enters into the contract and has a duty to give reasons

Stage 7   Within 21 days after entering into the contract the landlord serves a notice on all leaseholders and RTA that:
- Outlines reasons for awarding the contract to the particular contractor or states where these reasons can be inspected
- And if observations were made at stage 5 above by leaseholders or RTA, summarises those observations and sets out the landlord's response to them.

The landlord need not give reasons or reply to observations in writing if either of the following occurs:
- The contract is awarded to the nominated contractor
- The contract went to the lowest tenderer

Variation on the basic procedure for Qualifying Works under EU procurement rules for which Public Notice is required – Schedule 4 (Part 1)

Stage 1   Landlord serves Notice of Intention on leaseholders and RTA
- Describes works to be carried out in general terms or specifies where more details can be inspected if it is a complex project
- States the landlord's reasons for wishing to carry out the works
- States that the landlord is not inviting nominations of contractors because public notice of works is to be given
- Invites written observations
- Leaseholders have 30 days to reply

Stage 2   Landlord considers any observations before deciding whether to proceed.

Stage 3   If proceeding to seek tenders the landlord provides a notification of proposed contract statement to all leaseholders and RTA or states where the statement can be inspected.

The statement must include:
- The name of the proposed contractor and any connection (apart from the proposed contract) between them

- An estimate of the leaseholder's contribution
  (Where this is not possible an estimate of the total cost of the works to the premises must be given;
  where this is not possible a statement of the applicable hourly/daily rate must be given;
  where neither is possible the reasons why not and the date by which the information will be available)
- A summary of the observations received in stage 1 and the landlord's response to them

  And invite observations on the contract statement and give 30 days to reply.

Stage 4   If observations are received the landlord shall give his response to them in writing within 21 days of receipt to the person or persons who made the response, not to all leaseholders.

■ New procedure for qualifying works under a long term agreement, that has already been consulted upon or was entered into before the commencement of the regulations (eg Partnering Contracts) – *Schedule 3*

It is increasingly the case, particularly in the public sector, that works to premises are proposed within the framework of a partnering or PFI contract, which itself is a Qualifying Long Term Agreement. The fact that the QLTA has been consulted upon already does not excuse the landlord from also consulting in respect of the proposed works to premises, if the prescribed amount is exceeded.

The procedure to be followed is a much simplified version of the full procedure, and only allows leaseholders to comment on the proposed works.

The procedure should be used for qualifying works under qualifying long-term agreements that were entered into both before and after the commencement of the new regulations.

Note: *This procedure may be used by landlords that entered into long term contracts for works before the date of commencement of the regulations, as long as the qualifying works are carried out on or after 2 months from the date of commencement of the regulations ie after 31 December 2003.*

This means that the old s20 rules still apply to works carried out prior to December 31 2003 under agreements entered into prior to the commencement date of the regulations (31 October 2003).

Summary of the procedure

> Serve a Notice of Intention
> (with an estimate of costs)
>
> Allow 30 days for observations on estimates
>
> Respond to any observation to individual leaseholders only
> within 21 days of of receipt of observation

Details of the procedure

Stage1   Landlord serves Notice of Intention on each leaseholder and RTA

- Describes works to be carried out or where documents are available for inspection
- States the reasons why the landlord considers it necessary to carry out the works
- States the estimated expenditure/cost of the works
- Invites written observations
- Leaseholders have 30 days to reply

Stage 2   Landlord must have regard to leaseholders'/RTA's comments received in relation to proposed qualifying works and estimated expenditure.

If observations are received then the landlord shall reply in writing within 21 days of receipt giving his response, to the person who made those observations

It is important to follow these procedures carefully. Failure to consult in the proper manner may mean that costs above the prescribed amount cannot be recovered from leaseholders. If landlords do not follow the procedure or consult, then leaseholders may challenge the recovery of the cost at a LVT and only the sums up to the prescribed amount per leaseholder will be recoverable.

❑ 7.3 Consultation requirements on a change of leasehold management arrangements

One of the most significant implications of the new consultation arrangements is for local authorities contemplating new management contracts through ALMOs or PFI or other arrangements.

There are three considerations:

- Legislative requirements
- Contractual requirements
- Good practice requirements

■ The legislative requirements

Secure tenants have to be consulted about a change in management arrangements under s105 of the Housing Act 1985, and landlords have to take that consultation into account in reaching a decision. This does not apply to leaseholders, but it would be good practice to include leaseholders in the s105 arrangements, particularly as they may comprise a significant proportion of the affected residents.

Under s30B of the Landlord and Tenant Act 1985 (inserted by s44 of the Landlord and Tenant Act 1987) recognised residents' associations may obtain information and make representations about the appointment and employment of managing agents.

A recognised residents' association has slightly more powers of inspection and consultation than individual leaseholders, together with rights to appoint external advisors. Section 29 of the Landlord and Tenant Act 1985 grants leaseholders the right to form a residents' association to represent their interests. Residents may request recognition of a representative association by the landlord, who must reply within a reasonable time, and may not withhold consent unreasonably. Failing this, residents may request a certificate of recognition from the local Rent Assessment Committee. There are currently no specific requirements as to how a residents' association should be constituted, but if there is a body representing leaseholders on an individual estate, it should be included in the s105 consultation process.

■ Changes under the Commonhold and Leasehold Reform Act 2002

The Act introduces a new requirement to consult on service contracts of more than 12 months duration (to be known as *Qualifying Long Term Agreements – QLTAs*). The precise criteria for QLTAs are contained in the Service Charges (Consultation requirements) (England) Regulations 2003 SI No 1987 and described in the previous section of this guide.

With a comprehensive housing management contract, it is quite possible that leaseholders would be faced with charges arising from that contract of more than £100 per annum including VAT, which would require consultation with leaseholders to be undertaken in accordance with s20 of the Landlord and Tenant Act 1985 as amended by s151 of the Commonhold and Leasehold Reform Act 2002.

■ Contractual considerations

The landlord is also bound by any provisions in the leases concerning management arrangements, the use of managing agents, and consultation requirements.

It is unlikely that most leases will contain anything that restricts the landlord's ability to use a managing agent, but there may be provisions that limit the management fees that can be charged, and it would be as well to be aware of these before tendering. Certainly any reputable future service providers should satisfy themselves in this respect.

It is possible that leases contain consultation obligations, so this will need to be checked as well.

It is important also to check whether there have been any public commitments made – say in the last five years – about the management of housing generally, and about leasehold management specifically.

■ Good practice

It is sensible to include the leaseholders within the tenant consultation process under s105 of the Housing Act 1985, and allow for the leaseholders to have a least one meeting on their own. The landlord would be acting as a reasonable landlord to follow the same processes as for tenants.

The precise form of consultation to be undertaken under s105 of the Housing Act 1985 is not laid down, but court decisions based on other legislation suggest it means the provision by the consulting body of sufficient information to allow the person or body consulted to offer useful comments and advice.

The consulted body, or leaseholders, must be allowed a reasonable time to consider and formulate a response, and the consulting body must properly consider responses received. This does not mean that they must act in accordance with them, but a body wishing to avoid legal challenge on this point should ensure that it can, if challenged, put forward cogent reasons for its eventual decision and show that any responses it rejected were carefully considered.

Although not currently a legal requirement a reasoned reply to respondents, especially those whose advice is rejected, will greatly diminish the chance of a successful challenge. Under the 2002 Act reasons for the choice of contractor will have to be given if the leaseholders submitted observations on the tenders or nominated a contractor.

If the successful contractor is the leaseholders' nominee or the lowest tenderer, there is no obligation on the landlord to notify the leaseholders, but it would be good practice to do so.

Finally, it is a good idea to keep a record and copies of all documentation used in the consultation process. This will enable an audit trail to be followed in the case of challenges.

7.4 Emergencies and section 20 consultation

In emergency situations where there is no time to consult, landlords can be faced with difficult choices. Case law to date indicates that imminent physical collapse of a building is needed before the landlord can dispense with s20 consultation requirements.

The authority to dispense is transferred from the courts to LVTs under the Commonhold and Leasehold Reform Act 2002. Landlords can apply to LVTs to dispense with s20, but the delays experienced at present with obtaining a decision do not make this a practical option.

Landlords should send explanatory letters to leaseholders as quickly as possible if they believe there is a need to dispense with s20 procedures, giving reasons and setting out potential costs.

They will still need to obtain dispensation from the LVT, but the landlord will have taken all reasonable steps in the meantime.

....

Birmingham City Council approach to emergency works under section 20

Birmingham City Council informs leaseholders of the emergency works with a form of notice in compliance with s20(9) of the Landlord and Tenant Act 1985, which they have found of value if a leaseholder subsequently refuses to pay for the works or the council has to take court action to recover its costs.

....

❑ 7.5 Invoicing for major works carried out following section 20 consultation

Landlords adopt different approaches to the invoicing of major works – some will invoice separately and others as part of the annual service charge demand. If the lease defines major works as a service charge expense, which is generally the case, then *the only* invoices that can be sent are those provided for by the lease, which in most cases will be interim charges in advance and a balancing charge after the end of the year.

The new prescribed form of accounts under the Commonhold and Leasehold Reform Act 2002 that is expected in mid-2004 will require separate expenditure headings for s20 works and long-term contracts within the annual service charge statement.

It is true that invoicing separately for s20 expenditure allows easier monitoring of compliance with the 18 month rule, but inclusion with the annual service charge demand may be administratively simpler and provides the leaseholder with a single comprehensive picture of their liabilities, which will comply with legislation and most leases.

❏ 7.6 Further reading on section 20 consultation requirements

The Leasehold Advisory Service – LEASE – an independent advice agency funded by government grant – various information and guidance available – revised guidance and suggested form of notices issued, in conjunction with ARHM and ARMA on the new section 20 consultation requirements.
www.lease-advice.org.uk

Service Charges (Consultation Requirements)(England) Regulations 2003 (SI No 1987) issued as part of the Second Commencement Order August 2003
www.legislation.hmso.gov.uk

Also refer to Chapter 1.6 and 1.8 of this guide

CHAPTER 8

OTHER LEGAL CONSIDERATIONS FOR LEASEHOLD MANAGERS

This chapter deals with forfeiture, money judgements, resales and assignments, lease extensions and renewals and leasehold enfranchisement. It describes proposed changes to the law affecting conveyancing.

It considers the leasehold manager's role in supplying information to leaseholders who are selling their homes and recovering the costs of doing so.

It describes the procedures to be followed by landlords wishing to dispose of the freehold interest in leasehold blocks.

Finally, it briefly explains Commonhold as an alternative to the leasehold system and the right of leaseholders to convert to Commonhold in certain circumstances.

❏ 8.1 Forfeiture

Forfeiture means the ending of the lease and repossession by the landlord because the lease conditions have not been met. Crucially, it is without compensation therefore the leaseholder loses any equity remaining even after any debt has been repaid. This is why additional protection for leaseholders against forfeiture has been introduced in the Commonhold and Leasehold Reform Act 2002.

Legislation provides a range of measures to protect leaseholders, and where property is lawfully occupied as a dwelling, the landlord cannot recover possession of the premises without a court order.

The Protection from Eviction Act 1977 makes unlawful eviction a criminal offence with a maximum penalty of six months in prison and/or a fine of not more than £5,000.

Until the provisions of the Commonhold and Leasehold Reform Act 2002, described below, come into force, landlords can forfeit leases for non-payment of rent (which can include service charges depending on the wording of the lease) without prior service of any notices. The landlord still has to obtain a court order for possession and the tenant can apply for relief from forfeiture usually by clearing the debt.

However, a landlord may not exercise a right of re-entry or forfeiture for failure to pay a service charge unless the amount of the service charge:

- Is agreed by the tenant, or
- Has been subject of a determination by a court or by an arbitral tribunal in proceedings pursuant to an arbitration agreement (within the meaning of Part 1 of the Arbitration Act 1996).

In non-rent cases a landlord is required to serve a notice before exercising the right to forfeit the lease where terms of the lease have been breached by the leaseholder. The notice must specify the breach of the lease and give the leaseholder the opportunity to remedy it or to compensate the landlord for the effects of the breach.

Such a notice is served under s146 of the Law of Property Act 1925 before a court order can be obtained.

There are also a number of opportunities during the legal proceedings for the leaseholder to put matters right and avoid forfeiture of the lease.

The Commonhold and Leasehold Reform Act 2002 contains new provisions that place further restrictions on forfeiture. It is expected that it will not be possible to use forfeiture for debts (including rent, service charge and administration charges) of less than £350 unless the debt has been outstanding for more than a prescribed period (currently proposed to be three years).

These new provisions are expected to be brought into effect by a Commencement Order in mid-2004.

Landlords will also only be able to take action under s146 of the Law of Property Act 1925 when a court or LVT has determined that a breach of a covenant or condition of a lease has occurred, or the leaseholder has admitted the breach. Any notice of forfeiture cannot be served until 14 days after a final determination has been made.

It will not therefore be possible to use forfeiture in respect of other breaches of covenant unless the leaseholder has admitted the breach or a court or valuation tribunal has determined that a breach has occurred.

The new provisions will apply to outstanding debts of rent, service charges and administration charges. The objective is to prevent forfeiture for modest amounts unless they have been outstanding for an extended period. Administration charges for non-payment of an outstanding amount will not be taken into account in determining whether the prescribed sum has been exceeded.

The Act also introduces a power to prescribe additional or different requirements in relation to forfeiture. The Government intends to use this power to require landlords to take reasonable additional or alternative steps when there is no response to a demand or notice in order to protect absent or vulnerable leaseholders.

❑ 8.2 Money judgements

As an alternative to forfeiture proceedings in the case of unpaid charges landlords can consider obtaining a money judgement for the debt, through the county court, which allows the landlord to try and obtain the money that it is owed rather than obtaining possession of the property.

If the debt owed is below a certain amount the quickest and simplest way to obtain a county court judgement (CCJ) is via the Small Claims Court Track (SCT). Currently, the ceiling for cases to be heard under the SCT is £5,000, but this is reviewed from time to time. SCTs are dealt with at county courts.

To obtain a CCJ under the SCT, a claim form must be issued. These are usually obtained and prepared by the landlord's solicitors using information provided by the landlord. On completion, they are returned to the county court, usually that which covers the area where the leaseholder lives, along with the fee.

In April 2003 a new scale of fees was introduced starting at a minimum fee of £30 for claims up to £300, rising to £120 for claims of between £5,001 to £10,000.

The claim will be for a fixed amount, so subsequent arrears of charges would have to be the subject of a further summons unless they arose before the CCJ was given by the court.

Once the court receives the claim form, it issues the claim and serves a copy on the leaseholder and provides the landlord with a claim number. The leaseholder is given 14 days to respond, (although this can be extended to 28 days). If the leaseholder fails to respond the landlord can apply for a Judgement in Default (of a response). A CCJ is given against the leaseholder. If the leaseholder does respond to the claim form the court will set a hearing date for both sides to present their cases. At the hearing, the court will decide whether to give a CCJ for the debt owed. The landlord can ask for its costs to be met by the leaseholder. Most leases will contain a clause that allows the landlord to claim any legal costs incurred in recovering charges due.

If payment is not made in accordance with the CCJ, it can be enforced in a number of ways. These include enforcement by an attachment of earnings through the leaseholder's employer or the seizure of goods, by the court bailiff known as distraint.

Landlords can distrain for unpaid rent (except in assured tenancy cases) without a CCJ, but the Housing Corporation does not allow registered housing associations to do so, and the CIH also recommends that it is not used.

One of the main credit checks for mortgages, personal loans or credit cards is whether a person has, or has had, any CCJs. These usually remain on a court's records for six years. The threat of a CCJ may therefore prove an incentive to clear the outstanding debt, at least in some cases.

See also Chapter 9.1 – Charge collection from leaseholders.

❏ 8.3 Resales/assignments

■ Providing information to leaseholders wishing to sell

All leasehold managers are asked to supply information to leaseholders wishing to sell or to their solicitors. The request for information is usually received from the solicitor acting for the seller, but sometimes from the seller or the buyer.

The typical information requested is:
- The last three years' service charge accounts
- Details of the accounting year
- The latest service charge budget
- Details of insurance and ground rent
- Details of reserve funds held
- Any expected major expenditure planned
- Details of major works completed, but not yet billed
- Any consents for alteration or improvement given on the property
- Any other landlord's notices served on the property
- Details of any disputes about service charges on the scheme
- Details of any outstanding payments due from the leaseholder

The answering of such requests for information is often delegated to the scheme management team, or in larger organisations with a regular workload, to specialist staff. The ability to handle the requests depends upon having systems to keep the basic information accessible and requires the copying of basic records, but there will also be further requests and supplementary questions that will require judgement and detailed knowledge of the schemes.

The seller will rely on the answers given and so there is an obligation on the manager to give correct and up to date information.

In responding to solicitors' enquiries the landlord is obliged to answer truthfully but a clause in the reply letter or covering letter (if a form is to be returned) to the effect 'as far as the seller is aware' or 'to the best of our knowledge' should be included.

■ Charging leaseholders for the costs of providing information

It is quite normal for managers to make a charge for the information supplied. Both the RICS and ARHM codes do not consider this task to be part of the duties included in the basic management fee, and this view is given further authority under the Commonhold and Leasehold Reform Act 2002 with the introduction of the concept of administration charges relating to leases (see Chapter 5.14 of this guide).

Managers have adopted different ways to recover these costs.

- Some leases, often on retirement schemes, have a formula for charging as a percentage of the resale or purchase price. Such a formula will usually include any charges for consent and registration as well as for information plus supplying a leaseholders' handbook.

- Some managers charge a fixed fee for the standard information and identify for that figure what will be given. Any additional requests may attract extra charges.

- Other managers have a schedule of charges for different items of the standard information and the seller's solicitor can order which items are wanted – for example £40 for accounts, £75 for insurance.

Most leases make no reference to charges for this kind of information, so it is up to the manager to decide how to charge. In making a decision about charges managers need to be aware of the following.

- The RICS code of practice requires that managers have a 'menu' of charges for duties outside of the basic management fee.

- The ARHM code of practice requires that managers should not make any charge on resale except where it is stated or implied in the lease or where a service has been offered and accepted at an agreed fee.

- It is good practice therefore to have a publicly available statement of the charge or charges to be made. If the manager is registered for VAT, then VAT will also be chargeable.

- Any charge set should be reasonable because it is likely that the charges may be challengeable by the leaseholder at an Leasehold Valuation Tribunal. The 2002 Act introduced the right of leaseholders to challenge administration charges, including charges set as a formula in leases (see Chapter 5.14).

■ Changes in the law affecting conveyancing

The Government wishes to speed up the sales process for residential properties and several initiatives are underway of which leasehold managers should be aware.

Home Information Packs

In 2002 the Government announced its intention to legislate to make what were then known as 'sellers' packs' compulsory for residential properties. A seller would not be able to market a property until the information required in the pack had been obtained.

Home Information Packs are included in the draft Housing Bill that came before Parliament in March 2003. The precise contents will be defined in Regulations to be published after the bill has been enacted.

For leasehold flats this means that the seller or their solicitor will ask the manager for the usual information before the property goes on sale, rather than when a purchaser has been found. The same information will be required but at a much earlier date. It will also require that the information required from the manager is updated if there is a long delay from marketing until eventual sale.

The statutory sellers' pack obligations will not apply to sales to sitting tenants under the various rights to purchase, since such transactions do not involve marketing to the public. However the ODPM will be consulting on the scope for applying the sellers' pack principles to these types of sale as well.

The type of information that will be required in Home information Packs includes:

- Terms of sale
- Evidence of title
- Replies to standard preliminary enquiries made on behalf of buyers
- Copies of any planning, listed building and building regulations consents and approvals
- Copies of warranties and guarantees (new properties)
- Any guarantees for work carried out on the property
- Local authority searches
- Home condition report, based on a professional survey of the property, including an energy efficiency assessment.

And, specifically for leasehold properties:

- A copy of the lease
- Most recent service charge accounts and receipts
- Building insurance policy details and payment receipts
- Regulations made by the landlord or management company
- Memorandum and articles of the landlord or management company.

Electronic conveyancing

The National Land Information System is being set up as a one-stop shop for most of the legal information required in conveyancing. It will be accessed online and contain information from the Land Registry and local authority land charges, highways and planning departments. Also the law is to be changed to allow contracts to be transferred and signed by e-mail. The Land Registration Act 2002 and the Land Registration Rules 2003 have made substantial changes to land registration rules and procedures.

All these changes mean that conveyancing should speed up significantly. The impact on leasehold managers is that solicitors and sellers will expect them also to speed up their replies to requests for any information.

■ Notification of changes of leaseholder

Most leases contain clauses that require changes of leaseholder upon sale to be notified to the landlord, and what may be required of the landlord at that time. There are two legal terms applied to sales.

Assignment – is the sale of the remaining term of a lease by the leaseholder to another person who becomes the leaseholder. This is the most common way that leases are sold and assignment is often used to mean the sale of leases. Buyers are often called assignees.

Surrender – is the selling or giving up of the lease to a landlord by the leaseholder. The landlord pays the leaseholder a price for giving up the lease and then can sell a new lease to a new leaseholder.

Most leases are assignable, but surrenderable leases have been used in the social sector.

■ Consent to assign

Some leases require the prior consent of the landlord before assignment. Such consent has often been used in social housing leases because of particular restrictions.

For example, Right to Buy leases will require the repayment of discounts if disposals are made within the first 3 years and so prior consent may be required to ensure the discount is repaid.

Leasehold schemes for the elderly and shared ownership schemes for the elderly may be restricted to persons above a certain age, and sold at discounts which are to help those not as well off who could not afford to buy at full market prices. A typical retirement lease clause may be:

> "…not to assign or dispose of the dwelling as a whole except to an elderly person who is in the opinion of the landlord in need of sheltered housing in accordance with the criteria set out in the schedule hereto…"

Even if prior consent to assign is required from the landlord, then the landlord does not have a free hand in making a decision.

- Whether the lease says so or not, the landlord cannot unreasonably withhold consent (Landlord and Tenant Act 1927)
- The landlord must inform the leaseholder of the decision within a reasonable time
- And the landlord must give the reasons in writing (Landlord and Tenant Act 1988).

Further, the courts have decided that if a landlord does not give his reasons in a reasonable time or in writing then he/she cannot rely on any reasons brought up at a later date. Registered housing associations should refer to Housing Corporation guidance on disposals of land, following enactment of the Land Registration Act 2002. See Circular 08/03 on the Corporation website.

■ Deeds of covenant

Some leases require the seller to make the buyer enter into a deed of covenant with the landlord, a deed that commits the new leaseholder to abide by the covenants in the lease.

A typical clause may be:

> "Upon any assignment sub-letting or underletting (the leaseholder) to obtain a direct deed of covenant by the assignee sub-lessee or underlessee with the landlord to observe and perform the covenants and conditions of this lease and to pay the reasonable fees of the Landlord in connection with such assignment…"

In addition the form of the deed to be used is often in an appendix or schedule to the lease. The deed does not restrict consent to the assignment, but gives early notice to the landlord of the assignee. The purchaser's solicitor will prepare it and a copy will be sent to the landlord.

■ Notification of assignment

The third and most common way for the landlord to be made aware of new leaseholders is by notification of the assignment after sale. Note that a lease may require a combination of prior consent, deed of covenant and notification. A typical lease clause for notification may be:

> "To give to the solicitor of the landlord within one month of any assignment underlease or devolution or of parting with possession of the premises notice thereof in writing specifying the name and address of the assignee… And upon each such registration to pay the landlord a fee."

Law stationers sell standard notice of assignment forms and solicitors acting for the buyer to the landlord often send these to the landlord.

■ Surrender

Surrender gives the landlord greatest control over the new leaseholder, because it is the landlord who sells a new lease to a new leaseholder. However leases with surrender clauses are not normally mortgageable and so little used.

Some early leasehold schemes for the elderly used surrender clauses to control the sale of leases to older people, but such clauses have their own difficulties regarding timing of repayment to the seller, and payment of service charges and council tax once surrender has been accepted. It is possible for landlords to sell with new leases that are assignable to replace leases with surrender clauses, but generally legal advice should be sought first.

❑ 8.4 Repayment of discount and charges on RTB, PRTB and RTA leasehold property

Under s156 of the Housing Act 1985, if the leaseholder has obtained a mortgage for the purpose of purchasing the lease this becomes the first charge on the property and has to be registered at the Land Registry.

The second charge is for the repayment of the discount where one has been given. If however the leaseholder wishes to take out a further mortgage from one of the approved lending bodies for any of the reasons defined in sub-section 4 of s156, for example for their own improvements or for payment for service charges, this can then become the second charge thereby postponing the payment of the discount to the third charge.

❑ 8.5 Lease extensions and renewals

■ Flats

Leaseholders of flats have another legal right to enhance their ownership of their flats, without having to use collective enfranchisement. It is lease extension – the right to have the landlord grant a new lease for a term of 90 years, plus the present unexpired term, all at a peppercorn rent.

This right was introduced by the Leasehold Reform, Housing and Urban Development Act 1993 and has mainly been used in the private sector by leaseholders although it is also available to leaseholders in the social sector. The right tackles the problem of a short lease that is becoming a deteriorating asset for the leaseholder. Unlike collective enfranchisement, individual leaseholders can use the right without having to act as part of a group or form a company. A price has to be paid taking into account certain elements, but it is likely the price will be lower than the value added to a new lease in the longer term.

The right to a lease extension has been much simplified by the Commonhold and Leasehold Reform Act 2002, making it a more attractive option for leaseholders. Coupled with the right to manage, lease extension offers what is likely to be a simpler solution than collective enfranchisement to the common problems of leaseholders. Control over management can be gained by use of the right to manage; then a new extended lease can be sought individually by lease extension as suits the individual circumstances of leaseholders. Using collective enfranchisement to achieve these goals requires a group of leaseholders to act together and to collectively raise the finance for the purchase, which is always a difficult course to follow.

Leasehold extension has not been common in the social housing sector because most leases have been granted for 99 or 125 year terms starting in the 1980s. However, as these leases reduce towards 80 years remaining, there may well be more interest. The 2002 Act altered the price to be paid for lease extension such that marriage value is only paid if the unexpired term is less than 80 years, a cut-off point that will attract the interest of leaseholders and valuers.

Summary of rules for lease extension

- Most leaseholders qualify if they have owned their flat for the last two years and have a long lease, over 21 years. Shared ownership leaseholders have no statutory right to a lease extension, but the Housing Corporation supports the granting of extensions wherever it is practical to do so.
- It applies to most landlords including housing associations and local authorities. Charitable housing trusts are excluded if the flat is provided as part of their charitable purposes.
- If a leaseholder dies, the personal representatives who inherit have the right to apply also, and have two years from the date of the grant of probate to exercise their right to an extension.

Valuation procedures for lease extension

The principles are similar but not identical to collective enfranchisement. The valuation is not straightforward and both leaseholders and landlords should seek specialist professional advice.

The price payable will be the sum of:
- The reduction in the value of the landlord's freehold by the lease extension – for example the new lease is at a peppercorn so there is an immediate loss of any ground rent income to the landlord.
- 50% of any marriage value – any increase in the value of the lease because it has been extended. BUT marriage value is only payable if a lease has less than 80 years remaining.
- Any compensation to the landlord for any other loss arising to the block from the lease extension.
- The landlord's reasonable costs of dealing with the leaseholders' right, but not the costs of appearing at an LVT.

Procedure for lease extension

- Leaseholder has the right to obtain information from the landlord to be able to use the right.
- Leaseholder obtains a valuation and serves a notice on the landlord stating the price offered.
- Landlord has two months to reply and has a number of options:
  - accept leaseholder's right and the price offered
  - accept leaseholder's right and propose another price
  - state why leaseholder cannot use the right.
- If there are negotiations on the price a period of two months is allowed.
- After the two months either party can apply to a LVT to determine the price and any other issues.

❏ 8.6 Leasehold enfranchisement of houses

This applies to leasehold houses only, of which there are an estimated 865,000 in England, with 79% of these in the North of England (Survey of English Housing 1998/99).

Leaseholders of houses were given the right to buy their freeholds in the Leasehold Reform Act 1967. The right has been extended by other Acts, and the 2002 Act has simplified qualification and provided additional rights.

The qualifications for the right and valuation are complex and are not explained in detail in this guide. Landlords and managers should be aware that the right applies to all types of landlord, and to most leaseholders of houses if they have a long lease (over 21 years) and have owned the lease for two years. Shared ownership leaseholders in houses only qualify if they own 100% of the equity. Some leaseholders also have a right to extend their leases.

❏ 8.7 Collective enfranchisement

The right of leaseholders of flats to collectively buy the freehold of their building is contained in the Leasehold Reform, Housing and Urban Development Act 1993, but has been simplified and made less restrictive by the Commonhold and Leasehold Reform Act 2002.

Leaseholders of charitable housing associations, including exempt charities, are excluded from the right to enfranchise, but it applies to all other landlords.

The right can be exercised in any building of two or more flats where at least two thirds of the flats are held on long residential leases.

To exercise the right the leaseholders must form a Right to Enfranchise (RTE) Company and the number of leaseholders participating through membership of the RTE Company must equal at least half the total number of flats in the block.

All leaseholders in the building have the right to become members if they wish.

Regulations are yet to be made setting down the Memorandum and Articles for RTE Companies, so for the time being the rules remain as defined in the 1993 Act.

The Commonhold and Leasehold Reform Act 2002 also extends from the current 10% to 25% the non-residential space that a building may contain before the right ceases to be available. This will have the effect of drawing substantially more premises within the scope of enfranchisement than currently is the case.

■ Summary of the procedure for collective enfranchisement

- The leaseholders will act during the procedure in their own names, or they may nominate a third party as a purchaser. Once the requirements of the 2002 Act come into force, currently expected to be mid-2004, it will not be possible for leaseholders to nominate another person or organisation as the 'nominee purchaser'. They will then have to form a company called a Right to Enfranchise Company.

- Before starting the leaseholders can serve on their landlord a 'discovery notice'. The purpose of this notice is to ask the landlord for information about the freehold and other leaseholders that will help them decide if they qualify to proceed. Landlords have 28 days to reply to each notice.

- The bid to buy the freehold starts when leaseholders send the landlord what is called the 'initial notice'. This is the formal offer to the landlord to buy. It has to contain a lot of prescribed information and the price offered.

- Landlords have two months to respond to the initial notice and have several options:
  - Agree leaseholders have the right and accept the offer, or reject and suggest another price.
  - Explain with reasons why they think the leaseholders do not qualify.

- If the landlord has suggested a different price and other terms, time is allowed for negotiations.

- If terms are agreed the parties must enter into a binding contract within two months of the date of the agreement.

- If terms cannot be agreed either party can refer the enfranchisement to a LVT and ask the tribunal to decide the price and other terms.

■ The valuation of freeholds for collective enfranchisement

Although leaseholders have a legal right to buy, they have to pay a price that takes into account several elements. The valuation is complex and both the leaseholders and landlords should take professional advice. The 2002 Act simplified the valuation formula and so made enfranchisement of more interest to leaseholders.

The formula for valuation of the freehold can be summarised as follows:

- The value of the landlord's interest in the property (usually the value of ground rents).
- Half of any marriage value. Marriage value is the benefit arising when the freehold and leasehold interests in a block are in the same hands. If the leaseholders buy the freehold they could grant themselves new leases on extended terms that are of greater value than their existing leases. Note, however, no marriage value is payable if a lease has 80 years or more to run.
- Compensation for relevant losses resulting to the landlord from sale of the freehold – eg loss of any development value.

And landlords are entitled to their reasonable costs of dealing with the enfranchisement claim, other than costs of appearing before an LVT.

■ The position on mixed tenure estates after enfranchisement

When leaseholders enfranchise they purchase the freehold and with it the right to control the management of the block. So on mixed tenure estates where the landlord owns flats that are for rent, or where there are commercial premises, the law provides that the landlord has the right to a 999 year leaseback at a nominal ground rent of those flats or commercial premises, that are not occupied by long residential leaseholders.

If the landlord is a local authority or housing association then the leaseback is mandatory.

If the landlord is not a local authority or housing association, then there is a choice to take a leaseback or sell the interest in those flats or commercial interests to the persons buying the freehold. The landlord has to state his choice at the counter notice stage of the procedure.

❏ 8.8 Sale of freeholds

Freeholds can be bought and sold like other property, and landlords often sell the freeholds of blocks of flats. The sale of a freehold will include the block, subject to leases granted, common parts, and any ancillary property such as garages, car parking and gardens.

The sale of freeholds is common in the private sector but has been to date relatively unusual where the landlord is a housing association or local authority. However, the freeholds of some retirement leasehold schemes have been sold by housing associations where the blocks were no longer in geographical areas where they wished to concentrate their work.

Another reason why social landlords may consider sales of freeholds arises as a result of the Right to Buy. In smaller blocks subject to the Right to Buy a local authority or transfer association may end up with all flats sold on long leases. As landlord it has little interest left in the block except providing services to minimal common parts; the management of which may cost more than the fees chargeable, and the value of ground rent (typically £10 – 25 per annum) will hardly cover the cost of collection.

In these circumstances it may be sensible for a social landlord to consider selling the freehold of the block.

Broomleigh HA is a transfer association that actively seeks to sell freeholds of blocks where all the flats have been sold under the right to buy (or preserved RTB). The association first of all offers to sell the freehold to the leaseholders as a group, and only if they are not interested, will sell on the open market.

■ Right of First Refusal

The freedom of landlords to sell the freeholds of blocks of flats has been restricted by law, in order to protect the interests of leaseholders who may want to buy the freehold themselves. In essence the law requires a landlord who wants to sell the freehold to give the leaseholders the opportunity to buy it, before selling to anyone else. The landlord has to offer the freehold at the price he requires and the leaseholders, as a group, can accept or reject the offer.

The relevant legislation is in Part 1 of the Landlord and Tenant Act 1987, as amended by the Housing Act 1996.

A landlord failing to give the right of first refusal commits a criminal offence, punishable by a fine. If a purchaser buys a freehold and discovers that the leaseholders were not informed, the purchaser is also required then, retrospectively, to offer the right of first refusal. Failure to do so is a criminal offence, punishable by a fine.

Summary of the Right to First Refusal

- All leaseholders are qualifying tenants
- Qualifying leaseholders must own more than 50% of the flats in the block
- A block does not qualify if more than 50% is in non-residential use
- It does not apply to certain landlords including registered housing associations, local authorities and housing action trusts
- It does not apply if the landlord is selling the freehold or freeholds by way of sale of shares in a company
- The landlord has to serve a notice offering to sell the freehold on at least 90% of the leaseholders, including the price wanted
- The leaseholders have two months in which to decide whether to buy. More than 50% of the leaseholders must support the decision to buy
- This does not mean the majority of leaseholders have to pay for the freehold. One or any group can buy or they can nominate any person or body to buy on their behalf
- Leaseholders are **not** required to set up a company to buy the freehold
- There are other special procedures that apply if landlord wishes to sell at an auction

---

Although the right of first refusal does not apply to housing associations there are references to good practice of which they should be aware.

- For retirement schemes the ARHM code requires that housing associations should give leaseholders the right of first refusal as if the legislation applied.
- The sale of any freehold will usually require the consent of the Housing Corporation. The Housing Corporation has normally required that housing associations consult all leaseholders before disposing of the freehold of their homes.

Housing Corporation Circular 03/03 provides further guidance to registered housing associations.

❑ 8.9 Commonhold as an alternative to the leasehold system

Part 1 of the Commonhold and Leasehold Reform Act 2002 deals with a new form of tenure known as Commonhold. This provides for freehold ownership of residential and commercial units by a Commonhold Association, which owns and manages the common parts, and whose membership is restricted to the unit freeholders, which in some circumstances may include a developer. The Act contains the basic statutory framework, but the working details will be published in 2004.

A major difference of approach from leasehold tenure will be the standardisation of all the ownership documentation and rules of Commonhold Associations aimed at ensuring common practice across the tenure.

Commonhold is a voluntary system, which from commencement will be available to the developers of new buildings. It will also be possible for existing leaseholders to convert to Commonhold provided all those with an interest agree. They would need to acquire the freehold first together with any intermediate leases, and would require the consent of any mortgagees.

It is expected that Commonhold will make a slow start, but that once the ground is broken and a few schemes can be seen to be a success, others will follow rapidly, including the conversion of existing leaseholds.

One major obstacle to conversion is likely to be the effect on existing freeholders, who under current proposals will not be entitled to any compensation.

❑ 8.10 Further reading on other legal considerations for leasehold managers

Arden and Partington, Hunter and Redpath-Stevens *Arden and Partington on Housing Law* Sweet and Maxwell (loose leaf volume – cd and online – subscription service) www.sweetandmaxwell.co.uk

Driscoll, James *Housing Law and Precedents* Sweet and Maxwell (loose leaf volume updated quarterly – subscription service – contains many useful forms and other documents as well as case law) www.sweetandmaxwell.co.uk

LEASE leaflets:
Valuation for collective enfranchisement
Lease extension – getting started
Valuation for leasehold extension

Leasehold houses – your right to buy the freehold of your house – leaflet published by ODPM

Kruse, John (2002) *Recovering Housing Debt: A Legal Guide* Chartered Institute of Housing and Housing Corporation

CHAPTER 9

OTHER MANAGEMENT CONSIDERATIONS FOR LEASEHOLD MANAGERS

This chapter deals with charge collection and what can be done to assist leaseholders facing difficulties with payment.

It deals with anti-social behaviour and the granting of permission to leaseholders to undertake alterations to the landlord's property.

It goes on to offer advice on the structural and organisational arrangements that landlord organisations should consider to deliver an effective leasehold management service, and finally provides an overview of the approach to informing and involving leaseholders in the management of the blocks in which they live.

❏ 9.1 Charge collection from leaseholders

In the previous chapter the legal remedies available to landlords to obtain payment of charges were described. Landlords, particularly in the social sector will also wish to consider ways to assist leaseholders to make payments and avoid debt.

■ Assisting leaseholders in financial difficulty

It is important that staff managing leasehold property can advise leaseholders of the benefits that they can access if they are in financial difficulties. The CIH legal guide *Recovering Housing Debt* deals comprehensively with both the prevention and recovery of debt, and social landlords in particular will want to ensure that the same sources of money advice and debt counselling are available to leaseholders as to other tenants. Leasehold managers should be aware that some leaseholders may be eligible for assistance with their housing costs through Income Support or the Job Seekers Allowance scheme.

There are several ways in which the burden of service charges can be eased for leaseholders:

- This guide has already stressed the importance of avoiding wide variations in service charges from year to year by preplanning major works and occasional expenses. However, many landlords are already faced with situations where past failures to provide a sinking fund or to undertake stock condition surveys have meant that unforeseen costs will fall upon leaseholders.

- Right to Buy leaseholders, and to a lesser extent shared ownership leaseholders are likely to have lower incomes than other owner occupiers and are more susceptible to financial difficulties. Therefore it is important that landlords have a means by which they can assist leaseholders to cope with such situations.

Housing associations and local authorities have developed a range of hardship schemes to assist their lessees. Indeed, the Government has encouraged local authorities to develop hardship schemes and has allowed considerable latitude for them.

In developing their own hardship schemes local authorities are advised by the Government to consider whether assistance should be confined:

- to charges arising from major works of repair, maintenance or improvement; and
- to leaseholders with insufficient borrowing capacity to raise an interest bearing loan for the sum in question.

Where the local authority decides that part or all of a debt may be abated, appropriate provision will need to be made from the revenue account in accordance with good accounting practice.

- Some housing associations offer loans at no or low interest, and others allow delayed payment over a short period.
- Some leasehold schemes for older people have offered assistance by deferring payment until resale. Where this is done a legal charge on the property should be registered and interest charged.

Bromford Housing Group – service charge arrears prevention

The majority of the Association's leases allow for advance collection of a monthly budgeted service charge, and the Association is very focused on taking preventative action before the service charge falls into arrears. Some of the initiatives adopted have included:

- Completing budget summaries with customers on shared ownership leasehold properties to ensure affordability pre purchase
- Offering a home visit to explain service charges and the importance of keeping payments up to date, as soon as a new customer moves into a leasehold property
- Having a clear policy in place for service charge arrears and communicating this to customers in a simple leaflet format
- Taking prompt action for non-payment of arrears, including home visits
- Setting service charge budgets as closely as possible to actual expenditure to prevent shortfalls in budgeted service charge collection at the end of a financial year.

At the end of the financial year in March 2002 arrears were less than 1 % of total budgeted service charge.

Each landlord should consider this issue and decide on its policy. It will be influenced by the number of leaseholders and the circumstances surrounding the major works and the size of the bills.

It may be more appropriate to consider loan assistance for those with large bills and/or where the local authority leases have not allowed for sinking funds.

In practice, housing associations often offer significantly more discretionary assistance to leaseholders than do local authorities, particularly in respect of the costs of regeneration schemes. Associations are generally able to offer a range of buy back, alternative homes, interest free loans – and anything else that is needed to enable the chosen scheme to proceed, whilst local authorities are likely to shelter behind their wider fiduciary duties, and offer very little discretionary assistance to leaseholders. This can lead to the distinct possibility that no scheme at all proceeds in the case of demolition and redevelopment as the compulsory purchase process would be too prolonged.

■ Housing (Service Charge Loans) Regulations 1992 (SI No 1708)

Under the regulations Right to Buy leaseholders have the right to a loan from the landlord, or the Housing Corporation if the landlord is a registered housing association, within the first 10 years of their lease. Purchasers under the Preserved Right to Buy and the Right to Acquire do not have this right.

The conditions are:

- The total service charge demand in any one year is more than £1,900 (this would include contributions to major works)
- The current minimum amount of the loan is £640 and the maximum £25,250 adjusted annually by reference to the RPI
- Loans were only available for charges relating to repairs, but will now be available for improvements under the new definitions in the 2002 Act.

The amounts given relate to those set in the original legislation and these are uprated on an annual basis. The landlord has a legal duty to inform leaseholders of their right to a loan, advising leaseholders if the right will apply when sending a service charge demand.

■ Social Landlords Mandatory Reduction of Service Charges (England) Directions 1997

The Mandatory Directions *require* reduction of service charges for repairs, maintenance or improvements in certain circumstances (see Chapter 5.1 for further details).

■ Social Landlords Discretionary Reduction of Service Charges (England) Directions 1997

Under the Discretionary Directions, social landlords *may* reduce or waive service charges for past, current and future works of repair, maintenance or improvement in certain circumstances (see Chapter 5.1 for further details).

❏ 9.2 Anti-social behaviour and leaseholders

Tackling anti-social behaviour is a high priority for the government, local authorities, landlords and residents. The law has been developed and extended to provide new tools and powers to deal with individuals whose behaviour, in the terms of the Crime and Disorder Act 1998, causes harassment, alarm and distress.

Under the Anti-Social Behaviour Bill it will be a requirement of every local authority and housing association to have a published policy and procedures document dealing with anti-social behaviour.

Landlords that are public bodies may be challenged under the Human Rights Act 1998 if they do not take reasonable steps to ensure residents have quiet enjoyment of their homes.

The Government report *Tackling Anti-Social Behaviour on Mixed Tenure Estates* (April 2003) identifies the need for local Crime and Disorder Partnerships to effectively tackle problems of youth nuisance and anti-social behaviour, and that effective partnerships require:

* Knowledge of the nature of the problem
* The development of multi-agency partnerships
* The engagement of residents to build community capacity

Leasehold managers need to ensure that they contribute to the development of local initiatives to tackle anti-social behaviour.

■ Complaints by leaseholders about periodic tenants

On mixed tenure schemes, if a leaseholder complains about the behaviour of a tenant then the landlord's normal procedures for investigating complaints should be followed. If the complaint is found to be justified, action can then be taken in accordance with normal housing management policy. It should be noted however that some leases may require the leaseholder to take action themselves, or to fund any action the landlord takes on the leaseholder's behalf.

■ Complaints by tenants about leaseholders

Where the behaviour of a leaseholder is the subject of complaint by a tenant or group of tenants, the landlord's powers to act may be limited by the terms of the lease, and action to obtain forfeiture will only be possible where a proven and irredeemable breach of the lease has occurred.

The landlord has no special powers or responsibilities by virtue of its ownership of the freehold of the property, and in many cases will be limited to advising and assisting the affected tenants to take legal action under the Environmental Protection Act 1990 or through court injunctions.

However if the behaviour involves serious anti-social activity or harassment, social landlords may consider a range of non-tenure specific remedies (see the following section).

When a complaint about a leaseholder is first received, the lease should be checked to ascertain whether, if proven, the leaseholder's actions would constitute a breach of the lease.

The principles of investigation of complaints, attempting mediation, and advising on courses of action open to those affected should nevertheless be pursued in accordance with the landlord's normal policy.

Sometimes a complaint relates to the occupant of a flat that has been sub-let by the leaseholder. Each case will need to be treated on its merits, but as a general principle, the leaseholder is responsible for ensuring compliance with the terms of the lease, and therefore should be required to take action to enforce compliance with the terms of the lease by the sub-tenant.

■ Harassment and serious anti-social behaviour

Generally speaking, for social landlords, the initial action that should be followed in dealing with racial harassment, sexual harassment and harassment on grounds of sexuality or serious ASB (eg drug dealings, violence, prostitution etc) will be those normally used by the landlord in relation to rented tenancies. As with other complaints, however, the alleged perpetrator may be the leaseholder rather than a tenant, and the landlord's powers both to investigate the actions of a leaseholder and to deal with a leaseholder's unacceptable behaviour may be limited by the terms of the lease. It is therefore essential to check the terms of the lease and confirm the extent of the landlord's powers to deal with the matter.

Social landlords now have a range of non-tenure specific remedies to tackle anti-social behaviour, including Acceptable Behaviour Contracts and Anti-Social Behaviour Orders (ASBOs – which until recently were only available to local authorities). Registered housing associations can now apply for them under provisions contained in the Police Reform Act 2002. Local authorities can also obtain ASB injunctions under s152 of the Housing Act 1996 against anybody causing serious ASB on one of their estates (when the Anti-Social Behaviour Bill becomes law this power is likely to be extended to RSLs). Local authorities also have powers under s222 of the Local Government Act 1972 to take appropriate court action (eg injunctions) against persons in order to protect the interests of the public in their local authority area.

It is also possible to place covenants in leases forbidding certain types of behaviour and to ensure proper enforcement of existing covenants. Injunctions can be obtained preventing certain actions by individuals, and provisions in the Environmental Protection Act 1990 can be used to curb noise nuisance.

The Housing Corporation expects registered housing associations to have strategies in place to tackle anti-social behaviour (Regulatory Code 3.5d). This covers all residents, regardless of tenure. But the key message remains that prevention is best, and there are steps that can be taken by social landlords, such as use of neighbourhood wardens and CCTV, although of course the costs of these may be reflected in service charges and may not always be popular with leaseholders, if indeed they are chargeable at all under the terms of the lease.

■ The costs of court proceedings in cases of nuisance/harassment

Normally, leases provide that if the landlord is to take action on behalf of the leaseholder, the leaseholder will indemnify the landlord against any costs that the landlord incurs.

■ Dealing with domestic violence and self-neglect

Where landlords become aware of situations where a leaseholder or a member of their household may be at risk from another member of their household or themselves, the matter should be quickly referred to the appropriate agency, in most cases the Social Services Department, or to the police.

❏ 9.3 Dealing with requests for permission to carry out alterations

In general it is unwise to give leaseholders permission to carry out works that are of a structural nature which are the responsibility of the landlord. An exception could be requests to renew windows, although even here, if there is a planned replacement programme it is wise to withhold permission.

In most but not all cases, the landlord will be responsible for the frame, which is regarded as structural, but the leaseholder will be responsible for the window and the glazing. In these cases the landlord could grant permission to renew their windows providing this is done to a specification approved by the landlord and subject to the normal terms and conditions that may be imposed on carrying out works, including relevant planning or building regulation requirements.

Where permission is sought by the leaseholder to carry out window replacement a check should be made to see if the work is included in the landlord's own maintenance programme and if so the leaseholder should be told. They should be informed in very clear terms in writing that if permission is granted to carry out the replacement, they will still have to meet their proportion of the cost of window renewal work if the landlord carries out window renewal to the rest of the block in the future.

Broomleigh Housing Association v Hughes [1999]

The lease required the leaseholder to pay a stated percentage of the service costs incurred by the landlord. The landlord replaced all the windows in the block except those of the leaseholder's flat since he had already replaced them without consent.

Following arbitration initiated by the Independent Housing Ombudsman Scheme, which found that the previous landlord had exempted leaseholders in similar situations from contributing to those costs, it was held that the leaseholder was entitled to the same treatment.

Broomleigh took the matter to the High Court where it was held that the leaseholder was liable to pay his specified proportion of the costs as required under the lease though he did not directly benefit.

The court held that the waiver of the benefit of any covenant by a landlord (or his predecessor) cannot extend beyond the instance or the breach to which it specifically relates: see section 148 of the Law of Property Act 1925. Similarly, the fact that some tenants have obtained a waiver of the service charges could not create a right or a legitimate expectation that other tenants would be treated in the same way.

Where a service charge relates to the maintenance of common parts of property divided into flats, a tenant is not exempt from paying it because he does not use the common parts; such a conclusion would deprive a service charge condition from having any meaning.

If a leaseholder is seeking permission to build a conservatory or other extension and it is attached to the property it will be counted as part of the structure when completed and will have future maintenance implications for the landlord. Part of the conditions of any permission granted must include the agreement of the leaseholder to meet the future maintenance costs. As the undertaking will not be binding if the lease is assigned, a licence should be granted and this should be recorded on the land register.

• •

Portsmouth City Council has ensured that successors in title are bound to maintain alterations the Council agreed may be carried out, by granting a supplemental lease containing a leaseholder's obligation to maintain.

• •

The letter setting out the conditions for approval of the works should include this charging information. The landlord will still be responsible for the repair and maintenance of the item if it is their responsibility in the lease, even if the item was installed by the leaseholder, so it is important to ensure that any works for which permission is given are undertaken to a satisfactory standard.

It is common for landlords to charge a fee for providing permissions whether technical input is required or not. Permissions are not items covered by service charges, see Chapter 5.14.

Carrying out alterations without the landlord's permission is a breach of the lease, and successors in title can also be held liable for the breach and required to take whatever action the landlord considers appropriate to remedy the breach.

❏ 9.4 Organisational arrangements

■ Policy and corporate guidance

In deciding upon the most effective organisational structure for delivering leasehold management services, the main choices facing landlords will depend upon the size and geographical spread of the leasehold stock and its potential for growth and, in the case of social landlords, upon the existing service delivery structure for rented housing and the capabilities of information systems.

The organisational options available for landlords are therefore varied and there is no single best approach, but rather there are some general principles that should be followed.

Historically, one of the main underlying problems of leasehold management in the social housing sector has been the failure of landlords to recognise the need for specific policy and organisational development in respect of the tenure. Although there have been improvements in recent years, many leasehold managers still have difficulty in raising the profile of their work within their organisations.

A further difficulty is that even when leasehold management is adequately resourced in the housing management department, it may still be under-resourced in other parts of the organisation that also provide key services to leaseholders.

Where services are procured from another part of the landlord organisation it is essential that service level agreements are in place to ensure the cost effectiveness and proper performance management of that service.

It is important for social landlords to establish a level of corporate understanding and expertise in leasehold matters. The extent to which this expertise is developed in-house, or relies upon external advice, will depend on the size and complexity of the leasehold portfolio and on the size and structure of the landlords' organisation.

Even where leasehold managers are having difficulty in raising the corporate profiles of leasehold management, there are actions they can take to tackle this. The leasehold team at one housing association began reporting corporately on the level of costs that had become irrecoverable because maintenance teams had let contracts without ensuring time for consultation was built into the programme.

■ Developing policies and procedures for leasehold management

The difference in the contractual relationship with leaseholders, as distinct from periodic tenants, means that policies and procedures used by staff for managing rented homes cannot necessarily be applied unchanged to the management of leasehold property.

It is necessary for separate policies and procedures to be drawn up, or at least existing procedures modified for the management of leasehold property.

In addition, separate procedures will be required to cover activities that are specific to leasehold management only.

Headrow Housing Group

Headrow have developed a concise policy and procedure guide on dealing with the management of shared ownership arrears.

The policy and procedures give basic advice to staff on the management of arrears in shared ownership property including: regular monitoring; which housing costs may be met through Housing Benefit or Income Support for low earners and the unemployed; the use of the small claims court; liaison with the mortgagee, the actions they may take and what this means for the association; and the difficulties of using forfeiture.

The procedures include a range of useful standard letters from initial contact to those dealing with the forfeiture of the lease. Key points of the procedure are summarised in a helpful list of bullet points.

As well as the usual enforcement options, the procedure includes the option for shared owners to reduce their equity holding in the property, and in some cases to resell their share entirely and become a rent-paying tenant of the property.

■ Co-ordinating the organisation's policy work on leasehold management

In larger organisations where it is likely that more than one department will be involved in the provision of services to leaseholders, there is a need for a single focal point within the landlord organisation with overall responsibility for providing advice and the co-ordination of leasehold policy matters.

This co-ordinating role involves checking that effective procedures are in place to provide services and may involve a lead role in bringing departments and sections together to agree policies and approaches to leasehold issues.

With the severe demands in the public sector for strict programming of large scale regeneration schemes it can often be difficult for the leasehold manager to get higher levels of management in other departments to take seriously the strict timetables and limitations of s20 consultation, or the issue of demands within the 18-month time limit. There is a great need for a fully co-ordinated policy and approach to leasehold matters if the leasehold manager is not to be left isolated within the system.

■ Keeping up to date with changes in the law, regulation, guidance and good practice

Because of the complexity of leasehold law and its frequency of change it is vital to arrange for ongoing monitoring of legislative, regulatory and good practice developments as they specifically affect leasehold management. This monitoring should consider the implications of changes and identify the policies or procedures that need to be produced or reviewed in light of them. Online services are especially useful for keeping abreast of change.

■ Obtaining external advice or guidance where necessary

Leasehold law is complex, especially when a lease requires interpretation or the implications of legislation are unclear. Most landlords will obtain advice from their legal advisors on leasehold matters, but will still need the capacity to recognise when that advice is needed and how to use it most effectively.

It is unwise to assume that the organisation's general legal advisors will be sufficiently expert in leasehold matters to deal with everything that will arise, and it is worth identifying legal firms with the necessary expertise.

■ Monitoring performance

The development of performance indicators for leasehold management should be considered separately from those developed for rented housing management. Leaseholder surveys should be used to supplement statistical performance measures, and information gathered in this way should be included in annual reports to leaseholders.

■ Training and staff development

Training is required for all staff involved in leasehold management or whose work impacts upon leaseholders to ensure that they understand both the needs of leaseholders and the law that governs the relationship between leaseholder and landlord. The specialist needs of leasehold managers must not be overlooked when training programmes are being developed and in the case of social landlords where leaseholds may not be the majority customer group, particular attention should be given to ensuring that leasehold managers are included in wider corporate training initiatives.

■ Delivering guidance on leasehold issues – the organisational options for social landlords

Organisational options for providing this central policy guidance role include the following:

- Adding it to the workload of a central policy team dealing with housing management
- Having a 'dedicated' staff member within a central policy team
- (In smaller organisations) giving the responsibility to a senior manager within the housing department
- Creating a specific leasehold management team and allocating the policy work to a 'dedicated' staff member within it
- (If housing management teams contain a separate leasehold officer) adding the work to their other responsibilities.

It may also be possible to split the work between staff. Provided one senior member of staff retains the responsibility for an overview of leasehold issues and the tasks are clearly divided, this should not pose undue difficulties.

Whatever organisational approach is chosen landlords should have clear objectives for the leasehold management service, together with targets and sound performance management arrangements, supported by clear and documented procedures.

■ Administrative and systems support

Accounting systems and practices

The systems for service charges invoicing, and the receipting of payments, must be linked to the systems used to account for costs. Because administration charge invoicing is not accounted for within service charge systems and the costs they relate to may similarly fall outside the block and estate accounting systems, these too must be closely linked.

The form of accounting for costs and for providing this information to leaseholders must comply with legislative requirements, the terms of the lease, and recommended accountancy practice. This has a significant impact on many internal systems and their administration.

As seen in earlier chapters, leaseholders have rights under Landlord and Tenant legislation to request summaries of service charge accounts plus supporting information – whether they are part of a leasehold scheme or a sole leaseholder in a block of rented property. Under most leases they will only be liable to contribute to costs associated with their own block or estate.

Single block accounting is required so that costs can be easily identified for each leaseholder. A system of coding is also required that allows the costs of different components of works or services to be broken down in a way that matches the breakdown for service charging in accordance with the lease. These costs include, for example, day to day repairs to communal areas and those repairs which are the landlord's responsibility, major works, service contracts covering lifts etc, grounds maintenance and cleaning of communal areas and utility charges.

Audit Commission inspectors have already identified the weakness of some landlords' accounting systems that are not fully property based, and local authorities and housing associations can expect this to be an area that future inspections will continue to examine.

Accounts must be capable of being presented in the format required under the Landlord and Tenant Act if leaseholders request them, and in the prescribed format for regular statements under the Commonhold and Leasehold Reform Act 2002 once that is in force. Regulations are expected to be laid before Parliament in mid 2004.

The need for a housing stock database
In order to easily identify leasehold properties and those where sales are being negotiated, it is essential that the landlord organisation keeps accurate and up to date records of properties including details of those affected by planned major works or improvements.

Comprehensive maintenance records are also required and will assist in identifying future service charges for Right to Buy and Right to Acquire properties.

Information Technology implications
Computer systems are necessary to support cost centre accounting, service charge and ground rent billing, administration charge billing, and to maintain the stock database. Also details need to be held about leases and leaseholders, records of payments and addresses for correspondence etc.

The specific requirements of leasehold management need to be considered in any information systems reviews and strategy planning that take place within the landlord organisation.

Auditing of accounts

Under s21 of the Landlord and Tenant Act 1985, leaseholders have the right to request a summary of service charge costs. Section 152 of the Commonhold and Leasehold Reform Act 2002 will require landlords to provide this annually together with a statement of the leaseholder's rights and obligations. Where there are more than four dwellings these accounts must be certified by a qualified accountant who is independent of the landlord, except in the case of local authorities, who may use their own suitably qualified finance officer.

Some leases may require the accounts to be audited rather than certified, which implies an item by item independent examination of the accounts for the block concerned.

❏ 9.5 Information and consultation

Consultation and providing information are essential tools of good leasehold management. A key principle is the need to be clear about leaseholders' expectations and priorities. As leaseholders are paying for services it is only reasonable for them to be kept informed and consulted when changes occur or are planned.

In the social housing sector it is now common for residents' associations on estates or mixed tenure developments to want to include both leaseholders and tenants in consultation exercises, and landlords should in general continue to encourage this. It should, however, remain clear that there will be times when the interests of leaseholders and tenants will diverge and separate consultation may be required.

The interests of leaseholders and periodic tenants are not always the same, particularly when it comes to major works, where as a result of pressure for physical improvements to an estate by periodic tenants, leaseholders may be faced with large bills for their share of the costs. As the number of leaseholders grows on an estate, so the potential for disagreement between tenants and leaseholders grows.

For housing associations consultation with leaseholders will take different forms depending on the type of lease held and whether they live within a leasehold scheme or not. Consultation with individual leaseholders who previously rented their own home will be the same as for local authority leaseholders.

■ Provision of information

A leaseholders' handbook that is regularly reviewed is an excellent way of providing much of the background information that leaseholders should have, and can be used to set out the service charge procedures in detail, where nothing in the lease prevents this.

An annual report can be used to regularly update leaseholders, and to report on performance.

Regular newsletters can also be used to keep leaseholders informed of progress with major works schemes and other policy matters that the landlord is considering.

Information should be available in plain English and in other formats appropriate to the profile of the landlord's leaseholders including Braille, audio tape and other languages.

It is important to strike the right balance as the costs of information provision ultimately fall on the leaseholders through their service charges, so they must be seen as adding real value to the quality of service the landlord provides.

··

Colchester Borough Council

The Council has a very clear and comprehensive guide for leaseholders on all aspects of leasehold ownership.

The plain English summary of the lease is particularly helpful to both staff and leaseholders. The general layout and presentation is a very user friendly format for conveying a large of amount of complex information.

The guide is reviewed and updated by the leasehold working party and this review includes consultation to seek leaseholders' views on it.

The design ensures that information is well set out and easily accessible. Text is not cramped on the page; topic headings are clear and unambiguous. Good use is made of icons and boxes to divide up information and to highlight basic key issues or further advice/actions the leaseholder can take. Well thought out frequently asked questions are included as part of the text relating directly to the information being discussed in a helpful and relevant way. The language used is clear, straightforward and easily understood, avoiding the use of jargon.

The guide also provides a useful telephone listing of council services and other services and organisations such as the police, utility companies and citizens' advice bureaux, as well as grants and dealing with noise complaints.

··

■ Customer service standards, disputes and complaints

The organisation should have general customer service standards but these will probably need additional sections to cover leasehold management.

The complexity of leasehold management, and especially service charges, almost invariably creates queries and disputes. The organisation should have very clear lines of responsibility for all aspects of leasehold management. The leasehold management procedures should identify who deals with queries and disputes and indicate others who have a responsibility to respond to the person handling the query or dispute.

The organisation should also consider how the resolving of queries and disputes fits in with the formal complaints process.

These procedures should be publicised in a leaseholders' handbook.

Formal consultation agreements with leaseholders

One housing association has entered into two consultation agreements with leaseholders – one relating to retirement housing schemes and the other to shared ownership homes.

The agreement with leaseholders of retirement schemes covers:
- Arrangements for an end of year service charge accounts meeting at the scheme
- Arrangements for a budget presentation meeting to residents of each scheme
- Availability of staff to attend up to 2 other general meetings each year at the scheme
- A commitment to consultation on the replacement of equipment such as washing machines at the scheme
- A commitment to consultation in relation to resident manager recruitment
- A commitment to regular informal meetings between the resident warden and all residents
- The methods of consultation to be used including circular letters and individual consultation
- A commitment to consultation in relation to changed arrangements for emergency and mobile warden services
- A commitment to feeding back the results of consultation to leaseholders
- The role of scheme residents' associations
- Arrangements for section 20 consultation
- Consultation on sales policy and assessment criteria for new residents

The consultation agreements were developed with full input from leaseholders and the draft agreements were sent to many residents' associations and retirement schemes for comment before being finalised.

■ Residents' associations

Residents' associations should be encouraged, and efforts made to establish and maintain good working relationships with them.

It is important to remember, however, that consultation with a residents' association is just one mechanism for consultation and cannot replace consultation with individual leaseholders.

■ Recognition of residents' associations

It is sensible for landlords to have a procedure and criteria for recognising residents' associations. Without it, landlords can find themselves consulting with groups that may not be representative of the residents or may not be properly run.

The procedure set out in the Landlord and Tenant Act 1985 (as amended) is as follows:

- A residents' association can apply to their landlord to be formally recognised for the purposes of consultation under the Landlord and Tenant Acts

- The landlord must reply in writing to the secretary of the residents' association confirming that recognised status has been granted if the association meets reasonable criteria

- Alternatively the residents' association can obtain a certificate of recognition from the local rent assessment committee. This is not normally given unless the association has a membership of at least 60% of the leaseholders and a relevant constitution

- Recognition can be withdrawn by writing to the residents' association's secretary giving at least six months notice

- A residents' association qualifies for recognition as long as residents are contributing towards the same service charge costs

The ARHM code recommends recognition of residents' associations with a 50% membership, and AIMS issues model constitutions for residents associations.

The Residential Property Tribunal Service has also published a suggested constitution for leaseholders seeking recognition.

The Tenant Participation Advisory Service website www.tpas.org.uk offers guidelines on developing a constitution.

Suggested criteria for recognising a residents' association could include:

- It should have a written constitution
- It should be open to all residents to join
- It must notify the landlord of all members and officers who are entitled to speak for it
- Its membership should meet a defined minimum level of leaseholders (60% has been adopted by many social landlords)
- It should provide an updated list of members and officers at least annually to confirm that it still meets the criteria for recognition

In the light of experience, landlords may wish to have additional criteria but should avoid making them too onerous.

If a new residents' association meets the agreed criteria, the association should be advised that it is formally recognised and will be consulted in accordance with the landlord's code of practice.

■ Support for residents' associations

Some social landlords provide support to leaseholders' residents' associations in the same way as for tenants' associations. On some mixed tenure estates residents' associations may represent both tenants and leaseholders and be supported in accordance with the landlord's general policy on tenant participation.

Landlords should consider how best they can provide support to residents' associations, particularly whilst they are being established.

Forms of support could include the following, all of which are examples of support currently provided by associations or local authorities.

Support for residents' associations *may* include:

- Advice on how to get started and an explanation of the model constitution
- Staff attendance at meetings to assist new residents' associations
- Training for residents on how to organise and chair meetings
- Provision of a start-up grant to support new residents' associations. This can be a lump sum or an amount per member and is payable in the first year only
- Provision of an administration grant. This can be paid each year to support the running costs of the residents' associations
- Providing venues for meetings
- Providing basic administrative support eg typing and photocopying facilities

NB: The costs of providing the start-up and administration grants should be met from a resident participation or other central budget but not be charged against the cost of the scheme for service charge purposes unless the lease has specifically allowed for this.

■ Methods of consultation

Annual meetings

Whether or not a residents' association exists, it is good practice to hold an annual meeting on each leasehold scheme to present the service charge accounts and provide an opportunity for questions and comments. This can ultimately be less time-consuming for staff than having to deal individually with explanations and queries. It is particularly important where there is a significant level of service provided, such as with retirement schemes, but on any mixed tenure estate with significant numbers of leaseholders social landlords may wish to follow a similar procedure.

The ARHM Code of Practice requires its members to hold an annual consultation meeting.

Leaseholders' forum

The creation of a leaseholders' forum across the landlord's housing stock can be beneficial where there is a large number of leaseholders. A forum can be used to provide information and training and to discuss general issues regarding service delivery and management arrangements. Forums also provide a mechanism for leaseholders to exchange views and to discuss the services provided to them.

They are often set up with a representative from each scheme or estate, including residents' associations where recognised, and meet once or twice each year or to consider specific issues. It can also be linked to the landlord's wider consultation arrangements at area or borough wide level.

....

Birmingham City Council: Leasehold Liaison Board

The Council has 3,000 leaseholders, but spread across 1,500 blocks. The Council has therefore set up a leasehold Liaison Board and held public meetings in each constituency (11) inviting all leaseholders in that area to attend. At the meeting the attendees elected two representatives to represent them on the Liaison Board. The Board now comprises 22 members meeting monthly. Elections are held every two years.

....

Leaseholder surveys

The process of consultation on day to day issues will help landlords understand what leaseholders want. However, it is valuable to supplement this with general satisfaction surveys which can be used for example to find out:

- Views on the services received by leaseholders
- Satisfaction levels with new homes on leasehold schemes. This should be addressed within 6 -12 months of leaseholders moving in

Information from surveys can be used to improve services and change practices and procedures. Whilst a one-off survey is useful, it is better to organise regular surveys so that the impact of any changes made can be monitored. It is suggested that a survey should be carried out every two to three years.

As with all surveys it is important to be clear about the information required and to ask the right questions and in suitable language. Some social landlords have used specialist companies to carry out surveys on their behalf.

A code of practice on consultation

A code of practice is a useful way of setting out a clear statement of the landlord's intentions on consulting leaseholders. It should state what will be the subject of consultation, with whom and how, so that leaseholders and residents' associations will know what to expect.

If there is a leaseholders' handbook, the code of practice should be included in it. Otherwise, the code can be issued to all new and existing leaseholders. As with all codes, it will need to be reviewed regularly.

Leaseholder involvement in the landlord's decision making

Many housing associations encourage leaseholders as well as tenants to apply for shareholding membership of the association and to become members of area-based committees.

Headrow Housing Group

Headrow has developed a form of service level agreement setting out the standards of service and customer care which leaseholders can expect, including details of their level of involvement in contractor selection and undertaking minor repairs.

The agreement is a useful example of setting service standards for leaseholders, and the association has gone a stage further by aiming to find out what level of involvement leaseholders want regarding the management of their homes. As might be expected the main areas of interest for leaseholders relate to the upkeep of their homes and the cost of providing these services. Examples of the involvement agreed by the Association include:

- Maintenance contractors reviewed annually and jointly agreed by leaseholders and the Association
- Leaseholders decide on an annual basis whether they wish to retain the gardening contractor
- Residents' committees have a small budget from which they can order minor repairs

❑ 9.6 Further reading on management considerations for leasehold managers

The Chartered Institute of Housing (CIH) – professional body for those who work in housing – also produces publications and good practice guidance including the *Housing Management Standards Manual* – the Good Practice Unit offers online information for subscribers.
www.cih.org/gpu

The National Housing Federation (NHF) – Housing association trade organisation – also produces publications and good practice information
www.housing.org.uk

HouseMark – performance improvement service for housing organisations
www.housemark.co.uk

The Association of Retirement Housing Managers (ARHM) – for Code of Practice, revised edition due spring 2004, also good practice notes for members
www.arhm.org

The Association of Residential Managing Agents (ARMA) has a code of practice and provides information and guidance for its members
www.arma.org.uk

The Royal Institution of Chartered Surveyors (RICS) – professional organisation for Chartered Surveyors – produces Code of Practice for service charge residential management and other residential management information, including online bulletins
www.rics.org.uk

Cheviot Housing Association *Leasehold Enforcement Good Practice Guide* Tel. 0191 238 3800

Kruse, John (2002) *Recovering Housing Debt: A Legal Guide* Chartered Institute of Housing and Housing Corporation

Tackling Anti Social Behaviour in Mixed Tenure Areas ODPM Publications
Email: odpm@twoten.press.net or via the ODPM website
www.housing.odpm.gov.uk

Housing Corporation (2002) *(How) Are You being Served – Good practice guide to complaints handing in housing associations*
www.housingcorplibrary.org.uk

CPAG *Welfare Benefits and Tax Credits Handbook 2003/4* – for readers who want to look further into support with housing costs available to leaseholders
www.cpag.org.uk

CHAPTER 10

MANAGING AGENTS

This chapter examines the role of the managing agent, the types of agency contract including flat management companies, and the specific legal requirements with which managing agents and management companies must comply.

It refers to the codes of practice that exist for managers and the role of the company secretary.

Lastly it outlines the process for the creation of a Right to Manage company under the provisions of the Commonhold and Leasehold Reform Act 2002.

❑ 10.1 The nature of managing agents

In the social sector it has been the norm that the landlord (the local authority or the housing association) is also the manager. This is not the case in the private sector where the manager is often an agent working for the landlord or sometimes for another company responsible for the management of the block.

However, it is becoming increasingly common for housing associations to act as managing agents for third party landlords including resident management companies.

The use of agencies in the social sector is likely to increase for a number of reasons. The right to manage and right to enfranchise will introduce flat management companies made up of leaseholders that will be seeking managing agents. Arms Length Management Organisations (ALMOs) are in effect private companies that are the managing agent of a local authority.

For the manager working as agent, ultimately the extent of the role is set not just by the terms of the lease, but by the terms of any contract or agreement with the landlord, and by the instructions given by the landlord to the agent.

■ Management of blocks of flats in the private sector

Managed by an agent for the landlord	33%
Managed by an agent for the leaseholders	14%
Managed by the leaseholders themselves	39%
Managed by the landlord	14%

(Source SEH 1998/99)

■ Types of agency arrangement

The most straightforward arrangement is where the manager is appointed as agent by the landlord. The landlord may be a private individual, an independent company, or a resident management company (the freeholds of 24% of blocks in the private sector were found to be jointly owned by the leaseholders in the Survey of English Housing 1998/99).

Another more complex, but still common, arrangement is for the manager to be an agent of a company that is not the landlord. Typically a lease will have the landlord and a named flat management company to which the landlord delegates all management functions. Such leases are often called three party leases (landlord, management company and leaseholder). In such three party leases it is common for each leaseholder to be given a share in the management company, so the leaseholders take responsibility for management, but ownership of the freehold remains with the landlord.

■ Flat management companies

The common use of flat management companies as the vehicle for fulfilling leasehold management responsibilities has meant that managers, as agents, have had to extend their skills and knowledge. They need to understand how such companies operate, be able to advise residents on the responsibilities of running such companies, and often supply company secretarial services.

The two common types of limited company have both been used for management companies: company limited by shares, or a company limited by guarantee.

A company limited by shares means that some or all leaseholders hold a share in the company. The shareholders have their say in the running of the company, and normally when a flat is sold the share is transferred to the new owner.

A company limited by guarantee does not have shares – it has members, and normally membership is restricted to leaseholders. 'By guarantee' means the members have agreed to contribute to the assets of the company if it is ever wound up.

If the company is limited by shares, when a flat is sold the seller is usually required to complete and sign a stock transfer form. The buyer should pay stamp duty on the form and pass it and the old share certificate to the company. The directors then have to authorise the change to the register of members and issue a new share certificate.

If the company is limited by guarantee there is usually less work involved when a flat is sold, but the company usually requires a member to resign and then the company will give consent for a new member to join.

The use of companies limited by guarantee as a vehicle for leasehold management is set to increase. The Commonhold and Leasehold Reform Act 2002 requires all Right to Manage claims by leaseholders and Right to Enfranchise purchases of freeholds to use this form of company. Standard memorandum and articles are prescribed for these companies by regulation: The Right to Manage (Prescribed Particulars and Forms) (England) Regulations 2003 (SI 2003 No 1988) and The RTM Companies (Memorandum and Articles of Association) (England) Regulations 2003 (SI 2003 No 2120).

Flat management companies, although formed for a different purpose than typical companies, are subject to the same legislation, primarily the Companies Act 1985. The main requirements of the Act are that companies must file with Companies House certain information:

- Annual report and accounts
- Annual return
- Changes in directorships

Failure to send the required information is a criminal offence and the company could also be struck off the register.

❑ 10.2 Contracts for managing agents

A manager undertaking work as an agent, and any landlord or flat management company appointing an agent, should enter into a contract which sets out the duties expected of the agent and who decides what.

Common sense advice to any manager before becoming the agent for any block would be:

- Are the problems and issues raised by the landlord or flat management company ones I can solve? If not, walk away.
- Do not promise what you can't deliver.
- Have an agency contract that sets out fairly what is expected of the manager and of the landlord or the flat management company.
- Ask to see copies of the leases in use.

A typical contract would include sections on the following:

- A schedule of the services that the manager has agreed to perform, set out in detail. The schedule may also list the frequency of certain duties eg meetings with the directors of the company.
- Conduct of the manager. The manager should contract to abide by a relevant code of practice, and comply with the terms of the leases.
- Conduct of the landlord or flat management company (the 'client'). The client should contract not to issue instructions to the manager that would be in breach of the terms of leases, relevant codes of practice or legislation.
- Insurances. Who insures what? In particular, managers should contract to hold professional indemnity insurance at all times.
- Discounts, rebates and commission. It is recommended good practice (see RICS and ARHM codes) that the manager declares any discounts, rebates or commissions received for any part of the services to be provided.
- Handling of monies. Who will hold funds and in what accounts? What authority will the manager have to spend funds and deduct any fees?
- Fees, including the management fee and any extra charges for additional duties.
- Dispute resolution.
- Termination.

Model contracts suitable for managers and flat management companies are available from the RICS and the ARHM.

❑ 10.3 Codes of practice and the law for managing agents

Managers from the social sector, who are traditionally landlords as well, should be aware that their legal status changes fundamentally if they become agents for a landlord or flat management company not in the social sector.

The requirements of the Company Memorandum and Articles of Association must be observed. This is particularly important in respect of voting rights and the administration and conduct of meetings.

Social sector managers also need to be aware that RTM and RTE companies will be companies limited by guarantee. Managing as agent for a RTM or RTE company means that the agent is effectively a private sector landlord. The relevant Landlord and Tenant law and codes for the private sector will therefore apply.

- Exemption from s42 of Landlord and Tenant Act 1987 does not apply to social sector managers if they are agents. The exemption only applies as landlords and therefore as agents for a private sector landlord, or RTM

Company or RTE company, the manager must hold service charge monies in trust, and set up individual scheme bank accounts.

- Interest earned on service charge monies held in trust is liable to tax, a problem which social sector landlords may not have had to face before.

- Any management fees charged to the landlord will attract VAT at the standard rate. This will apply to any managing agent registered for VAT and so will include ALMOs.

The RICS Code of Practice becomes relevant if the block is not a special one for retired people. The ARHM Code of Practice becomes relevant for any retirement block.

Although an agent could ignore these codes, it would be inadvisable for the landlord or client company. Leaseholders dissatisfied with the management of the agent could use the code as a benchmark of good practice in evidence at a Leasehold Valuation Tribunal against the landlord.

❏ 10.4 The company secretarial role for managers

As explained above, flat management companies are subject to the same requirements as any other limited companies and must file the required records at Companies House, including accounts in the format for companies under company law rather than landlord and tenant law. Because many flat management companies run by leascholders do not possess the knowledge, time or skills to handle these matters, a lot of them fail to comply with Companies House's rules. Many have been struck off and dissolved, leaving management of the block in limbo.

Therefore flat management companies often seek agents who can offer the services of a company secretary to the flat management company, in addition to traditional leasehold management services.

The typical duties of the company secretary offered by a manager would include :

- Issuing membership or share certificates

- Arranging venues for AGMs and EGMs

- Preparing agendas for AGMS, EGMs, attending and taking minutes

- Filing statutory company returns

- Keeping registers of shareholders and members

- Keeping minute books of meetings

Taking on the company secretarial role for flat management companies is not a decision to be taken lightly. Effectively someone in the organisation will become an officer of one or more limited companies, and be responsible for the timely completion and return of company records. Failure to carry out the role can lead to fines and prosecution.

❑ 10.5 Statutory accounts for flat management companies

All leasehold managers are aware that blocks of flats should have annual service charge accounts produced as a matter of good practice. The Commonhold and Leasehold Reform Act 2002 requires a prescribed form for such accounts and makes them a legal requirement for all blocks.

However, flat management companies, because they are limited companies, must also prepare statutory accounts according to the Companies Act and other regulations. The two types of account are not the same, and failure to comply with the requirements of statutory accounts for a limited company can lead to prosecution of the directors.

The statutory company accounts must also be sent to Companies House within strict time limits, normally 10 months after the end of the financial year. There are fines if the time limit is missed.

Companies House strongly advises all flat management companies, even the smallest, to use the services of a professional accountant to prepare the statutory accounts. For leasehold managers this is an extra service that will normally be sought from them by flat management companies. Alternatively the manager may prepare the services accounts according to Landlord and Tenant law, and then pass it and relevant records to the company's nominated accountant.

Some small flat management companies exercise the option to file 'dormant' accounts, which are much simpler. Many can also take advantage of small companies exemptions and so do not require an audit of the company accounts.

In summary, a flat management company, and any RTM or RTE company will have to prepare the statement of account for the service charge and give copies to all leaseholders, as required by the Commonhold and Leasehold Reform Act. They will also have to prepare company accounts in a quite different format as required by company law.

The company must maintain a clear distinction between service charge expenditure and any expenses of running the company. Such company expenses must not form part of the service charge, unless provided for in the lease, which will not be allowed in the case of RTM and RTE companies.

❑ 10.6 Right to Manage companies

A description of the new Right to Manage (RTM) under the Commonhold and Leasehold Reform Act 2002 and the circumstance in which it can be exercised is found in Chapter 2 of this guide. The following paragraphs consider the mode of operation of the Right to Manage company and the implications for landlords and managing agents.

It should be remembered that the right exists for all leaseholders except those of local authorities.

■ Setting up a Right to Manage company

Leaseholders wishing to exercise the RTM must first set up an RTM company, which will be a company limited by guarantee whose objects must include the acquisition and exercise of the Right to Manage. The constitution must be in accordance with model memorandum and articles contained in The RTM Companies (Memorandum and Articles of Association) (England) Regulations 2003 (SI 2003 No 2120).

Any leaseholder with a lease with an original term of more than 21 years may become a member of the RTM company, as may the landlord once the RTM notice has been served, but not before. In order to prevent RTM companies competing for the management of a block, once one RTM company has registered no further registrations may be made.

Only one person from each flat can become a member, so joint leaseholders will have to agree upon this. In mixed use blocks, business leaseholders are excluded from becoming members, but the landlord will have voting rights.

The RTM exists for leaseholders of charitable housing associations, but it should be noted that shared ownership leaseholders will not have the right until they have purchased 100% of the leasehold equity.

The new RTM company must invite all leaseholders to become members by serving a 'notice of invitation to participate'. This notice is in a prescribed form set out in the Right to Manage (Prescribed Particulars and Forms) (England) Regulations 2003 SI 2003 No 1988.

❑ 10.7 Further reading on managing agents

Appointing a Managing Agent – a LEASE/ARMA leaflet available from LEASE www.lease-advice.org

Model agency contract for retirement schemes – available from ARHM, tel. 020 7820 1839.

Model agreement for the appointment of agents to blocks of flats – Available from RICS Books, tel. 01203 694757.

Cox, Nigel (1993, 4th edition expected 2004) *Running a Flat Management Company* Jordan Publishing Ltd ISBN 0 85308 8608

Companies House *Flat management companies*
ref GBA9 Tel: 0870 3333636

The Association of Residential Managing Agents (ARMA) has a code of practice and provides information and guidance for its members
www.arma.org.uk

LEASE leaflet on Right To Manage – available on website
www.lease-advice.org

CHAPTER 11

LEASEHOLD VALUATION TRIBUNALS

This chapter explains the jurisdiction and operation of Leasehold Valuation Tribunals, and the extension to their powers under the Commonhold and Leasehold Reform Act 2002.

❏ 11.1 Introduction

Since 1967 Leasehold Valuation Tribunals (LVTs) have been given various powers previously exercised by the courts. The Housing Act 1996 continued this process and significant further extension of their jurisdiction was introduced in the Commonhold and Leasehold Reform Act 2002, and was made effective by regulations published in August 2003: Leasehold Valuation Tribunals (Procedure) (England) Regulations 2003 (SI 2003 No 2099) and Leasehold Valuation Tribunals (Fees) (England) Regulations 2003 (SI 2003 No 2098).

LVTs are independent and impartial. They normally consist of three members: a lawyer, a valuer, and a layperson. Hearings are semi-formal and evidence is not given under oath.

Under the Housing Act 1996 LVTs have jurisdiction to determine:
- *Reasonableness of service charges:*
  Disputes involving service charges which may be either transferred from the county court for determination by the LVT or by direct application to the tribunal by either the landlord or a leaseholder.
- *Appointment of managers:*
  The Housing Act 1996 transferred the jurisdiction for the appointment of managers from the courts.
- *Reasonableness of insurance:*
  Disputes involving insurance taken out by the landlord may also be resolved by the LVT.

and jurisdictions regarding valuation for enfranchisement and lease extension under the 1967 and 1993 Acts.

❑ 11.2 Changes to the jurisdiction of LVTs under the Commonhold and Leasehold Reform Act 2002

The jurisdiction of LVTs is widened significantly so that they can deal with most kinds of disputes about service charges.

Under the 2002 Act LVTs are able to determine whether or not a service charge is payable, including:

- The person by whom it is payable
- The person to whom it is payable
- The amount that is payable
- The date at which it is payable
- The manner in which it is payable

This new jurisdiction applies to charges already paid and charges that are proposed, so the *Daejan* case noted in 11.4 below will no longer apply.

LVTs are now able to:

- Consider administration charges and determine both their reasonableness and the reasonableness of any formula in the lease to arrive at them
- Vary leases that do not make adequate provision in relation to various matters including service and other charges (previously a jurisdiction of the county court)
- Award costs where in the opinion of the tribunal a party has, in bringing or conducting proceedings before the tribunal, acted frivolously, vexatiously, abusively, disruptively, or otherwise unreasonably

LVTs will still not be able to consider a matter where the leaseholder has already agreed or admitted the charge, but the fact that they may have made payment no longer signifies their agreement with it.

Appeals against LVT determinations to the Lands Tribunal are now only allowed with the permission of the LVT or the Lands Tribunal.

These powers came into force from 30 September 2003.

The changes are a very significant extension of the powers of LVTs. The only significant matter that will remain outside their jurisdiction is a leaseholder's right to set off and counterclaim for disrepair.

❑ 11.3 Arbitration

Landlords should always consider the use of mediation and arbitration, which may save both parties time and money. Some local authorities have set up local leasehold arbitration schemes.

The LB Southwark Leaseholders' Arbitration Panel

The Panel comprises one councillor, an independent chair and a leaseholder and hears applications from leaseholders who are still dissatisfied after using the Council's formal complaints procedure.

The panel has the power to:
- 'Declare as to the rights of a party'
- Reduce the level of service charges
- Make awards up to a maximum of £350
- Require either party to carry out certain tasks such as works
- Require council officers, contractors and others to attend the panel
- Award damages but not compensation.

The panel is able to arbitrate on the sales process, service charges, major works and breaches of the terms of the lease.

Leaseholders have to sign an agreement to be bound by the rules and the decision of the panel, but they are still free to exercise their right to take any dispute to court for settlement.

❑ 11.4 The reasonableness of service charges

Section 83 of the Housing Act 1996 amended s19 of the Landlord and Tenant Act 1985 (as amended) and added a new section (s31A) which gives LVTs jurisdiction to determine applications from either the landlord or tenant on the reasonableness of service charges.

The LVT is able to consider:
- Whether costs incurred for services, repairs, maintenance, insurance or management were reasonably incurred
- Whether services or works for which costs were incurred are of a reasonable standard
- Whether an amount payable before costs are incurred is reasonable

This applies to variable service charges as defined by the Landlord and Tenant Act 1985, which include costs already incurred and costs still to be incurred for items such as management, cleaning, gardening, entryphone, maintenance and insurance. Also covered are reserve funds for both cyclical works and long term sinking funds.

Although a Court of Appeal ruling *Daejan Properties Ltd v London LVT [2001]* determined that LVTs only have the jurisdiction to decide the reasonableness of disputed service charges that are still unpaid, their jurisdiction has now been extended under the changes contained in the Commonhold and Leasehold Reform Act 2002 to include charges already paid (see also 11.2 above).

Landlords are able to seek a ruling at proposal stage, if they wish to be certain that their plans are reasonable before they start spending. However, as LVTs have tended to find in favour of leaseholders, landlords may wish to carefully consider the merits of using LVTs to resolve service charge disputes.

Many service charge disputes revolve around interpretation of the provisions of the lease or compliance with consultation requirements under the Landlord and Tenant Act 1985, and LVTs have historically been unable to make determinations in respect of these matters.

❑ 11.5 Appointment of a manager

Since 1996 LVTs have had the sole jurisdiction in respect of the appointment of a manager where:
- Unreasonable service charges have been or will be made
- The landlord has failed to comply with a relevant code of practice, ie the RICS and ARHM Codes

Any leaseholder wishing to apply for an appointment of a manager must:
- Serve notice on the landlord giving the landlord the opportunity to remedy any breaches of covenant
- Advise the landlord of any requirements that need to be complied with for a stay in the action
- Specifying the grounds on which an order will be sought and how the grounds will be established

Where the landlord fails to take action the matter may be referred to the LVT or the county court for determination.

The LVT has the power to appoint a manager if it is satisfied that any one of the following grounds are proven:
- There has been a breach of the terms of lease
- Unreasonable service charges have been made or are likely to be made

- There is a failure to comply with the RICS or ARHM Codes
- Other circumstances exist which would justify the appointment

When deciding to appoint a manager the LVT will ask the applicant leaseholder to nominate a manager, whom they will then assess. The LVT will issue an order setting out the exact management functions that the manager is appointed to do. The appointed manager is responsible to the LVT.

LVTs do not have jurisdiction to appoint a manager where the landlord is the Crown, a local authority or other public sector body, a registered social landlord or other housing association. However, special rules apply when the Right to Manage is exercised.

The 2002 Act also has extended the ability to seek the appointment of a manager to leaseholders under three party leases.

❏ 11.6 Determination of reasonableness of insurance

The LVT may also be asked to determine whether an insurance premium or cover provided is reasonable, where the tenant is required to insure with an insurer nominated by the landlord.

Section 83 (2) of the Housing Act 1996 empowers a tribunal to order a landlord to use a different insurer where it can be shown that cover is inadequate or premiums excessive. The fee for a determination under s83 (2) is £300.

This jurisdiction only exists where leaseholders are required to arrange and pay for the insurance of their individual dwelling. It does not apply where the landlord arranges the insurance (eg for a whole block of flats) and recovers the costs from the tenants as part of the service charge.

Where the cost of insurance forms part of the service charge an application must be made for the determination of reasonableness under the procedures in Chapter 11.4 above.

❏ 11.7 The operation of LVTs

■ Procedure

There are no prescribed forms, but the Leasehold Advisory Service (LEASE) has produced an information pack, which includes standard forms that have been approved by the Government.

Individuals or groups of tenants may make applications and provide the following for the tribunal:

- A copy of the lease
- Names and addresses of those contributing to the service charge
- The current service charge payable and whether the tenants consider the charges to be reasonable
- The determination that is required from the LVT
- The name and address of any representative, the applicant and the landlord
- Whether the applicant intends to apply for a determination under s20C for the costs to be limited

LVTs are not able to consider matters where both parties have already agreed to arbitration.

■ Fees

In the case of applications relating to:

- Liability to pay service charge or administration charge
- The amount of the insurance premium
- The variation of leases because of administration charge

the fee is calculated by reference to the value of the application.

Where the service charge, insurance premium or administration charge which is the subject of the application, as follows:

(a) Is not more than £500, the fee is £50

(b) Is more than £500 but not more than £1,000, the fee is £70

(c) Is more than £1,000 but not more than £5,000, the fee is £100

(d) Is more than £5,000 but not more than £15,000, the fee is £200

(e) Is more than £15,000, the fee is £350

In the case of applications relating to:

- Dispensing with consultation requirements
- The suitability of a proposed insurer
- The appointment of a manager
- The variation of leases

the fee is calculated by reference to the number of dwellings to which the application relates, as follows:

a) Where the application relates to 5 or fewer dwellings, the fee is £150

b) Where the application relates to between 6 and 10 dwellings, the fee is £250

c) Where the application relates to more than 10 dwellings, the fee is £350

Applicants who are in receipt of benefits are exempt from these fees; the costs are levied pro-rata where some of the applicants are exempt and some are not.

Where a case has been transferred from the county court, any fees already paid towards court fees are counted against the LVT fees.

When an application has been made, the tribunal may appoint one member to examine the papers at a pre-trial review, which parties may or may not be invited to attend.

Once the pre-trial review has taken place, directions will be given to each party stating the information which the parties are required to provide and exchange prior to any hearing taking place. A date for a hearing would normally be set at this stage. Hearings are designed to be informal so that professional representation will not necessarily be required. Experts may be called where the parties wish, and expert witness statements should be exchanged in advance.

It is usual for inspections of the properties to take place during the morning of the hearing, with the hearing itself taking place during the afternoon.

Whether or not a pre-trial review is held, the tribunal may issue directions to the parties relating to the submission of evidence. Directions may well include time limits by which statements and documents have to be filed with the LVT, defining the issues which are in dispute and agreeing any facts that are not.

Where leases enable a landlord to recover legal costs within the service charge, a leaseholder may ask the tribunal to determine that the costs arising from the LVT are not charged to the leaseholders through the service charge, under s20C of the Landlord and Tenant Act 1985.

■ Appeals

Appeals against an LVT decision may only be made to the Lands Tribunal with the leave of the LVT or the Lands Tribunal itself. Applications for leave to appeal must be made within 21 days of the determination.

❏ 11.8 The future of the tribunals system

The Government has stated that in addition to the changes in the 2002 Act other steps are being taken to ensure that LVTs provide a better quality service for landlords and leaseholders.

In 2002 the administration of the work of LVTs was transferred to the newly named Residential Property Tribunal Service (RPTS), which operates from five regional offices. A new senior president was appointed to set national standards for the operation of the LVTs.

The Law Commission report *Land, Valuation and Housing Tribunals* was published in November 2003 and proposes a unified tribunal structure aimed at making the system more independent, coherent and user friendly. The proposals include a single generic Property and Valuation Tribunal (PVT) to hear the majority of first instance cases including those currently coming before existing Leasehold Valuation Tribunals. However, legislation will be required to bring the recommended changes into force.

❑ 11.9 Further reading on Leasehold Valuation Tribunals

Applying to a LVT – ODPM leaflet HC 200

Residential Property Tribunal Service (RPTS) – an independent body which gives an accessible service to landlords, tenants and leaseholders either to Rent Assessment Committees or the Leasehold Valuation Tribunal – various information and booklets can be downloaded
www.rpts.gov.uk

The Leasehold Advisory Service (LEASE) – an independent advice agency funded by government grant – various downloadable leaflets and information and guidance available including details of LVT decisions
www.lease-advice.org.uk

Gallagher, Stan (2003) *Leasehold Valuation Tribunals: A Practical Guide*
Sweet & Maxwell ISBN: 0421691301
www.smlawpub.co.uk

The Law Commission *Land, Valuation and Housing Tribunals: the future*
(Law Com 281)
www.lawcom.gov.uk/files/lc281.pdf

Glossary of Terms Used in Leasehold Management

Administration charges
Administration charges are amounts payable by leaseholders but not included in the service charge, such as for granting approvals for subletting or providing information or documents upon resale.

ARHM
Association of Retirement Housing Managers.

Arbitration
Settling a dispute by using a referee. If a dispute goes to arbitration it is settled by an independent referee. It avoids having to use the courts to settle the dispute.

Assignee
The person acquiring a property right by an assignment.

Assignment
The transfer of a property right from one person to another.

Breach
When an obligation in the lease is broken.

Case law
Law that is based on the results of previous court cases rather than legislation.

Commonhold
The freehold ownership of residential and commercial units by a Commonhold Association whose members are restricted to the freeholders of the individual units, which owns and manages the common parts.

Companies House
The office which stores company information such as annual accounts, directors' names and addresses and the registered office address. People who are interested in a company can inspect some of the information stored.

Completion date
The date a property transfers to the person buying it.

Consideration
The price paid for a promise given (need not be money).

Conveyance
A signed document which transfers land from one person to another.

Counterpart lease
An exact copy of the lease.

Covenants
Legally binding obligations and responsibilities.

Deed
A legal document which commits the person signing it to something.

Demised premises
The definition of the property being leased.

Designated reserve fund
Another name for a sinking fund which has been set up to hold monies collected by way of a service charge to meet the costs of future major works – it can be for a specific matter or for major repairs generally.

Determine
To end or decide.

Disbursement
A payment made by a professional person, such as a solicitor or accountant, on behalf of a client. The money is claimed back by including it on the bill for professional services which is sent to the client.

DIYSO
Do It Yourself Shared Ownership.

Easement
A legal right over someone else's land.

Enfranchisement
The legal right to buy the freehold of the property being leased.

EU Public Procurement Rules
Public Procurement is the term used in the European Union to describe the purchasing of works, supplies and services by national, regional and local public bodies, including central government, local authorities, fire and police

authorities, defence, health services, joint consortia of public bodies, and public and private utilities.

Exchange of contract
Swapping identical contracts between parties when land is sold; the person selling and the person buying both sign identical copies of the contract and exchange them. The contract is then binding on both of them.

Foreclosure
A lender repossessing a property because of the borrowers arrears.

Forfeiture
Ending of the lease and repossession by the landlord because the lease conditions have not been met.

Freehold
A form of tenure giving full ownership of land for all time.

Grant
Transferring the ownership of property.

Ground rent
Ground rent is a fee paid by the leaseholder to the freeholder as a condition of the lease. It is usually a small amount (such as £50 or £100 a year). Many leases don't specify an amount, but simply refer to a 'peppercorn rent'.

Group repair scheme
The external rehabilitation of groups of properties under the Local Government and Housing Act 1989 to prevent their deterioration (previously known as 'enveloping schemes').

HM Land Registry
A registry with offices in towns and cities throughout the UK which keep records of registered land.

Implied term
A term which is not written into a lease, but is assumed because of the actions of the parties, or which must be assumed if the contract is to work.

Indemnify
Compensation given by an individual to someone suffering a loss because of their actions.

Initial period
Five year period from the grant of a right to buy leasehold.

Interim charges
Advance payments of service charges.

Itemised repairs/works
Works that are specified in s125 notices.

Joint and several liability
Two or more people responsible for repaying a debt. They are each responsible individually to repay all the debt as well as being responsible as a group.

Lease
The document which creates the leasehold containing all the rights and obligations of the landlord and the leaseholder – a contract between the owner of a property and tenant, giving the tenant sole use of the property for an agreed time.

Leasehold
A form of tenure which gives the owner possession of the property for a substantial period of time which is clearly defined in the lease agreement (see term of years below).

Leasehold schemes for the elderly
Schemes developed by housing associations with the benefit of 30% Housing Association Grant, with the aim of helping less affluent purchasers.

Lessee/leaseholder
The person(s) with the lease of the property.

Lessor/landlord
The person/organisation granting the lease.

Life cycle costing
A method by which the cost of maintaining and modernising property can be estimated over its projected life. This enables long term planning of expenditure to take place, and service charges to be evenly spread over many years through the use of sinking funds.

Major works
There are many ways to define major works. For the purposes of this guide it relates to works costing more than the amounts prescribed in s20 of the Landlord and Tenant Act 1985 for consultation purposes, as amended by the Commonhold and Leasehold Reform Act 2002.

Management audit
In this guide management audit refers to the right given to leaseholders under s76 of the Leasehold Reform, Housing and Urban Development Act 1993 to undertake a management audit to satisfy themselves that the landlord is administering service charges effectively and efficiently.

Management fees
The fee charged by the landlord in accordance with the terms of a lease to cover their costs of management, as distinct from the costs of particular services such as cleaning, repairs etc.

Marriage value
In enfranchisement, marriage value is the extra value brought about by the freehold and leasehold interests being under the same control. These interests are often worth more together than apart.

Mixed tenure estate
An estate with both tenants and owner occupiers, some of whom may be leaseholders residing on it.

Mortgage
A loan which gives property as security.

Mortgagee
The person/organisation lending money to someone to buy a property.

Mortgagor
The person borrowing money to buy a property.

Non-itemised repairs
Works that are not explicitly defined in a s125 notice.

Parties to a lease
The landlord and lessee, and sometimes the management company.

Periodic tenancy
For the purposes of this guide the term is used generically to describe the secure and assured tenancies granted by social landlords, to differentiate them from leaseholds. A periodic tenancy means that the period of the tenancy runs from rent payment to rent payment. The notice period for a tenant to end a periodic tenancy will be a period equal to that of the rent period, except when the rent is paid weekly. In this situation the period will be at least 28 days. The notice to end the tenancy must also normally expire at the end of a period of the tenancy.

Precedent
Lower courts have to follow the decisions of the higher courts. This is called precedent, binding precedent or judicial precedent.

Provision
Where the lease allows something to be done.

Qualified surveyor
The term used in legislation to describe the person undertaking an examination of the landlords service charging arrangements under s76 of the Leasehold Reform, Housing and Urban Development Act 1993. It could in fact be a qualified accountant, valuer or surveyor.

Quarter days
In England and Wales the days when payments which are made every quarter should be paid. The quarter days are the days that the seasons are said to start. The actual dates and their names are:

> 25 March – Lady Day;
> 24 June – Midsummer Day;
> 29 September – Michaelmas Day; and
> 25 December.

Quiet enjoyment
Allowing a tenant to use land or property without interference. When a tenancy is created the landlord is expected to allow the tenant to use the land without any interference, unless the tenancy agreement allows it.

Recognised residents' association (RTA)
A residents' association recognised for consultation purposes under s29 of the Landlord and Tenant Act 1985.

Redemption
Paying off a mortgage/loan.

Reference period
A period of five years running from the date by which the landlord expects that a purchase under the right to buy will have been completed.

Registered Social Landlord
Not for profit organisation, registered with the Housing Corporation, providing housing and other services as defined in the Housing Act 1996. Housing associations still retain their statutory identity under s1 of the Housing Associations Act 1985.

Registered office
The official address where documents can be served on a company.

Repairing obligations
The repairs, which under the terms of a lease, the leaseholder and landlord each agree to undertake. There are therefore leaseholders' repairing obligations and landlords' repairing obligations.

Reservations
Rights which a seller of land keeps.

Reversion
The landlord's right to possession of a flat when a lease comes to an end.

Right of way
A legal right obliging the owner of land to allow authorised people to cross it.

Section 20 notice
A notice served under s20 of the Landlord and Tenant Act 1985 in respect of proposed major works.

Section 125 notice
A notice served under s125 of the Housing Act 1985 on a tenant exercising their Right to Buy, Preserved Right to Buy or Right to Acquire. The notice sets out, amongst other things, an estimate of annual service charges, all known structural defects and a description of current and future capital works to be carried out within five years.

Section 146 notice
A notice served under s146 of the Law of Property Act 1925 in order to obtain forfeiture of a lease.

Service charge
The charge made to the leaseholder for the provision of services under the lease.

Shared ownership
Purchase of a property in instalments. Purchasers buy an initial share from a housing association and pay rent on the part they do not own. Further shares are purchased (staircasing) until 100% of equity in the property is owned by the purchaser. Equity levels are capped in some rural developments and some schemes for the elderly.

Sinking fund
Collection of advance payments of service charges to fund future major repairs. Sometimes called a reserve fund – it can be for a specific matter or for major repairs generally.

Sub letting
Where the owner of a leasehold grants a tenancy (or a smaller lease) of the property.

Superior landlord
Where an association or local authority is not the freeholder but head leaseholder, or immediate landlord, the freeholder is known as the superior landlord.

Surrender
To give up a lease or legal interest.

Tenure
How a piece of land is held by the owner (for instance freehold or leasehold).

Term of years
Length of the lease.

Terms of a lease
Individual obligations or rights.

Title
Owning land.

Title deeds
The documents which prove who owns a property and under what terms.

Transferee
The person something is transferred to.

Transferor
The person who transfers something to someone else.

Underlease
The lease of a property granted by the leaseholder of the property to someone else.

Voluntary Purchase Grant
Voluntary Purchase Grant was introduced by the Housing Corporation in March 1996 to provide grants to existing tenants to purchase their own homes from housing associations choosing to participate in the scheme.

INDEX

Major entries shown in bold; Gl indicates Glossary